PRACTICAL SOCIAL WORK
Series Editor: Jo Campling

BASW

Editorial Advisory Board:
Terry Bamford, Malcolm Payne, Patrick Phelan,
Peter Riches, Daphne Statham, Jane Tunstill,
Sue Walrond-Skinner and Margaret Yelloly

Social work is at an important stage in its development. All professions must be responsive to changing social and economic conditions if they are to meet the needs of those they serve. This series focuses on sound practice and the specific contribution which social workers can make to the well-being of our society.

The British Association of Social Workers has always been conscious of its role in setting guidelines for practice and in seeking to raise professional standards. The conception of the Practical Social Work series arose from a survey of BASW members to discover where they, the practitioners in social work, felt there was the most need for new literature. The response was overwhelming and enthusiastic, and the result is a carefully planned, coherent series of books. The emphasis is firmly on practice, set in a theoretical framework. The books will inform, stimulate and promote discussion, thus adding to the further development of skills and high professional standards. All the authors are practitioners and teachers of social work, representing a wide variety of experience.

JO CAMPLING

PRACTICAL SOCIAL WORK

Series Editor: Jo Campling

⟨BASW⟩

Social Work and Child Abuse

David M. Cooper

and

David Ball

MACMILLAN

First published 1987
Reprinted 1989

Published by
MACMILLAN EDUCATION LTD
Houndmills, Basingstoke, Hampshire RG21 2XS
and London
Companies and representatives
throughout the world

Printed in China

British Library Cataloguing in Publication Data
Cooper, D. M. (David Michael)
Social work and child abuse.—(BASW practical social work)
1. Child abuse—Services—Great Britain
I. Title   II. Ball, David   III. Series
362.7′044   HV751.A6
ISBN 0-333-36397-3 (hardcover)
ISBN 0-333-36398-1 (paperback)

For Hilary and for Sylvia

Contents

List of Abbreviations

BASW   British Association of Social Workers
DHSS   Department of Health and Social Security
NSPCC   National Society for the Prevention of Cruelty to
                 Children
SSD   Social Services Department

Introduction

Much has been written about child abuse since it was first identified as a 'modern' problem in the 1960s. Writers have sought to isolate the nature and causes of abuse and specific methods of preventing or treating it.

Much less has been written about the unique role of local authority social workers in child abuse. They have been criticised, sometimes savagely, in a succession of formal enquiries into the deaths of abused children in their care or under their supervision. The net effect may be that local authority social workers have come to feel guilty, anxious and desperate as well as hungry for solutions to the difficult problems they face.

A practice guide for child abuse work is overdue but writing it is an almost impossible task. How to deal with a problem whose nature and definitition changes year by year? How to work within a formal legal setting which requires that children be protected? How to work within local government agencies which are large and bureaucratic? How to reconcile these pressures with the ethos of social work training which promotes helping, compassion, co-operation and respect for individuals whether they be children or parents? These are the dilemmas for the writers of a practice guide in child abuse for local authority social workers.

This guide offers no easy answers, no precise and detailed methods. Rather it attempts to maintain *perspective* and an acknowledgement that local authority social work will always be a compromise between a number of competing roles and tasks. It also distinguishes between infrequent complex acts of abuse in families across the social spectrum which may be almost impossible to predict and the more common catastrophies that occur in those families who are all too familiar to local authority social workers. In these latter cases, a theme of this guide is that there are no sophisticated and distinctive methods that have been particularly successful. They are more likely to respond to thoroughly developed child care skills that combine authority with a willingness to work with, as well as on behalf of, the community.

The themes in this guide may not immediately seem neatly practicable but in the long run we hope that our reluctance to offer magic answers will reassure social workers that they can do a difficult job well by acting on sound, basic principles of practice. While it is written primarily with the needs of local authority social workers in England and Wales in mind, we hope it will prove helpful elsewhere and in other contexts.

DAVID M. COOPER
DAVID BALL

1

Developments, Definitions and Reactions

Any book on child abuse should begin with some definitions of the topic. However, there are strong reasons, in our view, why this is not possible in anything but the broadest sense. Child abuse as an aspect of human social behaviour must be seen in its proper historical and sociological contexts and these are both complex. A thorough analysis is not possible in a practice handbook and we would refer readers to Parton's *The Politics of Child Abuse* (1985) for both its text and extensive references.

Again, it is not possible here to give more than a flavour of the vast range of research that has centred around child abuse. A Canadian work edited by Cook and Bowles (1980) is recommended for the many important authors and studies it includes. In England, the Open University team (Lee, 1978, Carver, 1978) provide concise but extensive reviews of trends in thinking and research, and the NSPCC have, since the late 1960s, produced much literature on everything from statistics on incidence to at-risk registers and methods of work with abusing families.

The expanding field

Between 1965 and 1985 the literature on child abuse multiplied enormously, first in America and then in England. The very changes of label, from child battering, through non-accidental injury to the present child abuse, suggest that tomorrow's discoveries will make today's definitions inade-

1

quate. Sexual abuse as a concept was little mentioned until
the late 1970s but it is now of major concern. The effect of so
much exploration and preoccupation has not been to clarify
the topic as much as to discover even more facets of it.

The paediatrician Alfred White Franklin has recounted
(1983) how in 1973 he was having difficulty persuading
publishers to accept a book which brought together the views
of 'The Tunbridge Wells Group' of workers – doctors, social
workers, police, magistrates – who were key figures in
publicising concerns about ill-treatment of children. In
particular they were in contact with American pioneers
especially Kempe. The publisher's doubts were quickly and
dramatically resolved by the death of Maria Colwell and the
subsequent official enquiry (DHSS, 1974a) which had the full
backing of the then Secretary of State for Social Services. The
book was published (Franklin, 1975) and the Tunbridge
Wells Group has continued to work at the centre of concern in
England about child abuse.

The Colwell enquiry was one of the first of about twenty-
five such, most of which have been summarised in a DHSS
publication (DHSS, 1981). The whole topic of enquiries is in
fact a sub-field of its own which has attracted much comment.
A British Association of Social Workers Report (BASW,
1982) registered great anxieties about procedures which can
cost as much as half a million pounds each and which can
adopt the manner of adversarial courts, lay blame and
perhaps raise more anxiety. The DHSS itself has issued more
major circulars about child abuse than about any other
specific area of social work. Social Services Departments,
(SSDs) themselves, in conjunction with other agencies, have
produced relevant guidelines and instructions with the kind of
detail that marks them out from other areas of work.

Child abuse is now truly international. 1976 saw the
founding of the International Society for the Prevention of
Child Abuse and Neglect (ISPCAN), followed in 1978 by the
British Association for the Study and Prevention of Child
Abuse and Neglect (BASPCAN). International conferences
now attract hundreds of attenders and almost as many papers.
Franklin, from his key position in this movement, summed up
such developments in 1983:

In the last decade we have seen the subject of the physical battering of children widen to include emotional battering, neglect, sexual abuse, sexual exploitation or prostitution, pornography, institutional mishandling and child labour. (Franklin, 1983a)

In the same paper he suggested that, for workers in such a field, the natural allies have become the World Health Organisation, the International Labour Organisation, the United Nations Children's Fund and the Anti-Slavery League.

The tendency to extend fields of interest is a very profound human urge. We can welcome the obvious concern about children's welfare but we can also ask whether 'more' automatically means 'better'. Writing about the explosion of conferences and research in child abuse in American Bergman asked questions about the distribution, in four years, of approximately $59 million in grant funds and said sadly, 'if few abused children benefited one can hope at least that the Dow-Jones averages gained a few percent!' (Bergman, 1980, p. 84). The important question in this, as in so many other fields of social welfare, is whether we might be reaching the point of diminishing returns and whether, instead, it is time to consolidate.

Incidence and statistics

Chisholm has said, 'There are no accurate figures for the incidence of child abuse in Canada' (Chisholm, 1980, p. 367). Gelles argued in an American context 'in other words there is no objective behaviour (short of murder or self-evident torture) we can automatically recognise as child abuse' (Gelles, 1980, p. 342). These assertions indicate the problems of definition that arise in the dynamic field of child abuse. To use an analogy it may be sensible to cast a net widely to catch as many fish as possible but only as long as we have the strength to pull it in. Definitions have both broadened and softened and this has meant that uncertain methodology, criteria for recording, the influence of reporting agents, the effects of labelling and skewed samples all complicate the picture.

There are important questions to be asked about any estimates of child abuse:

- Do they lump together children of different ages?
- Do they distinguish between abuse caused by relatives, careers and others?
- Do they only show offences known to the police?
- How big are statistical samples?
- Are figures set in an historical context (to measure trends)?
- Are figures set in a sociological context (to show what else is happening in a given society at a given time)?
- Are they based on actual incidents or on second-hand reports?

Child killings

In general, homicide of all kinds rose in England and Wales between 1948 and 1984 with the latest ten-year period showing an increase by one third over the previous ten years. Within this pattern there is no evidence from criminal statistics that child deaths stand out from the rest of the population (Home Office, 1984, pp. 58 and 67). If we narrow the focus further it does not appear that children are at increased risk of being killed by their parents or other family members. In fact, such detected offences declined between 1974 and 1984, although the actual numbers are so low that it is difficult to assert trends. For example, only 67 sons/daughters of all ages were killed by their parents in 1984 (Ditchfield, 1986, p. 39).

The NSPCC have mentioned detailed information centrally about abused children known to them in local offices. Creighton's 1984 study for the Society concluded that child deaths declined in the period 1977–84. However, the study group represented only about 10 per cent of the total child population of England and Wales and with only 36 deaths over the six-year period extrapolation is difficult (Creighton, 1984, p. 4).

Beyond basic statistical information there have been many

attempts to calculate the 'real' number of children killed. Because such enquiries face a variety of methodological problems, the estimates produced have been as varied as their authors. The following have all had wide publicity at different times with their numbers for annual child killings:

Hall	757	(Hall, 1975, p. 10)
Smith	450	(Smith, 1975, p. 33)
Oliver	300	(Oliver, vol. I, p. x and vol. II, p. 159)
NSPCC	50	(Creighton, 1984, p. 6)
NSPCC	150–200	(NSPCC, 1985, p. 4)
Beckford Report	40–50	(NSPCC, 1985, p. 289)

Child killing remains very difficult to estimate. As such it is dangerous to speculate, as the NSPCC have done, that their work may well have reduced the incidence (Creighton, 1984, p. 34), and difficult as well to assess the effects of greatly increased public concern and agency vigilance since 1974. Either greater attention can expose more cases of child killing or it can avert it. The former view has not been borne out in criminal statistics as it has in the case of rape, which during the 1980s has shown how a change in social attitudes can influence discovery and subsequent court prosecutions.

Perhaps there are two views of child killings. Either they resemble other forms of extreme domestic violence and are, therefore, uncommon and largely unpredictable, or they are much more frequent than we think. The problem with the latter view is that it still lacks sound or useful evidence to support it.

Child injuries

Children and injury are frequent companions. It has been estimated that as many as 65 per cent of children between 18 months and 3 years will show signs of recent minor accidental injury and studies of accidents in the home show clearly that children grow up surrounded by threats to their health (Home Accident Survey, 1982).

As in the case of deaths, information about deliberate

injuries to children is available either from broad criminal statistics or from smaller more detailed studies. Each source has obvious limitations with the added complication that whereas death is indisputable, there are difficult decisions to be made – by police prosecutors, doctors, social workers, even neighbours – about the gravity of injuries they may discover. A further difficulty is that the United Kingdom has no system of compulsory reporting laws of child abuse and this is unlikely to change if the recommendations of the latest DHSS-sponsored working party (1985a) are followed. The result is that detailed and reliable statistics of child abuse are not available.

Criminal statistics for England and Wales reveal an increase in violent offences averaging 6 per cent per annum between 1974 and 1984. Ditchfield's analysis (1984, p. 40) refers to the number of individuals found guilty or cautioned for cruelty to or neglect of children in 1984; this was higher, at 126, than in 1983 (103), but little different from the average for the period 1977–84. On the other hand, the numbers of children in care of local authority social service departments as a result of ill-treatment or neglect (as defined by Section I 2(a) of the Children and Young Persons Act 1969) rose steadily through the late 1970s and early 1980s. This will be discussed in more detail later.

More detailed estimates stem mainly from the NSPCC, and Creighton's studies concluded that for the period 1977–84, killings and serious injuries reduced while moderate injuries rose (Creighton, 1985). A study by Oliver in 1983 looked very closely at 560 children in North-East Wiltshire over a 21-year period and concluded that 513 of them suffered varying degrees of maltreatment, including 41 non-accidental deaths (Oliver, 1983, pp. 115–17)

Sexual abuse

It is perhaps more a moral than a legal question whether sexual abuse should be distinguished from other child abuse, except in its extreme forms. As a result, estimates of its incidence are not easy. Social attitudes towards sexual matters are notoriously fickle and cannot, therefore, consider the position of children separately from wider concerns – about rape, pornography, contraception, AIDS and teenage sex.

What is clear is that during the 1980s there has been much more concern, allied with (? or because of) extensive media interest, about the sexual abuse of children; as we show below in discussing pressures on welfare agencies, referrals of sexual abuse allegations rose spectacularly from very low levels during the 1970s. However, national crime statistics do not mirror this concern. Hence, 'over the period 1974–84 the numbers recorded in most classifications of sexual offences fell progressively. . . . An important exception to this pattern was the number of offences of rape recorded which increased steadily throughout the period' (Home Office, 1984, p. 27).

Apart from the offence of gross indecency against children which was introduced into statistics from 1983, other offences do not normally classify victims. Unlawful sexual intercourse with girls under 13 years and 16 years respectively fell between 1974 and 1984, the latter group from 4746 to 2633; common sense tells us that greater social tolerance of 'under-age' sex will have accounted for much of this reduction. Yet, incest offences fell overall from 337 to 290 during the same period, even though they now receive wider publicity (Home Office, 1984, Table 2.9, p. 39).

Beyond the criminal statistics the picture for child sexual abuse is dangerously confused. Kempe and Kempe's most recent book acknowledged the problems not only of definitions but also of incidence which they described in some categories as 'sometimes meager'; later they admit 'it is presently impossible to give accurate estimates of the total incidence of sexual abuse in the United States'. However, soon after, 'between one and two million women in the United States have been victimised by incest' (Kempe and Kempe, 1984, pp. 10, 13 and 17).

In the United Kingdom there is much less information about possible incidence and this is discussed in a 1984 CIBA Foundation publication. What is available comes mainly from incidents of sexual abuse recalled by adults. In the same way, a survey (MORI, 1985) of approximately 2000 persons aged

15 years and over concluded that about 10 per cent of them recalled some form of sexual abuse against themselves.

The present extent of abuse

Official statistics do not bear out any impression that England and Wales is suffering an epidemic of child abuse. As far as killings are concerned the numbers recorded are too small for making assertions, particularly from small samples. Although injuries yield higher figures, these bring their own difficulties. Firstly we must always take account of the social context which may vary from time to time. Reactions to rape illustrate this very well. Secondly, and this is the central problem in child abuse analysis, definitions of 'injury' have been dynamic rather than static so the framework within which any assumptions are made is far from clear. What is evident is that less people are being convicted of killing their children than in the past. Whatever the reason, this is a heartening statistic. Sceptics might argue that child killers now hide their crime better, but set against this is the undoubted fact that the public is now much more aware of child abuse than ten years ago and thus more likely to report it.

It should also be clear that any search for child abuse information is hampered because national statistics are sketchy. Inadequate categories, the different locations of data and the gap between government and other studies make it impossible to build up a valid and reliable picture. One can ask why it should be, after so much public concern, that in the UK the government has not yet devoted the same concerted effort to child abuse as it has, for example, in the case of either drug abuse or AIDS.

The 'disease' versus the 'generic' definition

It follows that if we cannot easily estimate the extent of child abuse then information about the kind of people who commit abuse is equally difficult to interpret. Despite considerable research over twenty years, we are not aware of any list of abuser characteristics that have much predictive value for individual cases and which, therefore, can be used by social workers as a checklist.

Definitions owe much to a 'disease model' of child abuse. This approach conceives of a syndrome, a discrete cluster of characteristics as might be found in a medical illness. Parent or caretaker characteristics would form the cause of the abuse within what Sheppard (1982, p. 2) describes as an 'individualistic pathology' framework. Similarly, Parton concludes that:

> When this model is applied to child abuse, it is assumed, therefore, that child abuse is an illness of sufficient unity to be put into a diagnostic category of its own right and that the pathology resides primarily in the parents, but manifests itself in the relationship with the child (Parton, 1985, p. 132 and also ch. 6).

Both Sheppard and Parton developed detailed criticisms of the disease model. These are twofold: firstly that such a model can only be a partial definition because it tends to exclude those wider environmental factors – poverty, housing, poor services, for example – which may well have an important effect on families. Secondly, even if the first criticism is rejected, the model is fundamentally deficient because abuse itself has been so loosely defined. The continuous 'discovery' of new forms of abuse has made the syndrome so wide that it is now virtually synonymous with 'poor child care' – a definition which is no longer distinctive or manageable as a specialist area of work.

For local authority social workers faced with massive increases in child abuse referrals, the problem of definition is not merely of academic interest; their need is for specific clues to specific problems and to date, these are not available. It is instructive to compare and contrast the position of child abuse knowledge with that of AIDS. In a very short time, the latter has been identified as a specific illness with distinctive characteristics; major progress has been made both in discovering causes and in developing treatment. This is not the case with child abuse where the major development has been intense worker anxiety and confusion, yet an expectation that an answer can be found.

The notion that child abuse may be merely an extreme form of poor child care is not necessarily a bad thing in our view. It implies, in fact, that things can go wrong in families for many different reasons and that appropriate social work should, therefore, be broadly and soundly based. In later chapters we develop this theme that there are no specific magic answers to child abuse; rather that good child care work is built on basic skills of role awareness, investigation, family assessment, risk-taking, inter-personal communication with children and parents and mobilising resources within family environments.

Social services and abuse

The previous section excluded referrals to welfare agencies as part of the data on child abuse; this is because, quite simply, an allegation is not the same as a proven incident. Both authors have experience of working within social service departments in 1974 and 1985 – a time of intense public alarm following the deaths of Maria Colwell and Jasmine Beckford respectively, which led to enormous pressure on social workers. In the latter case, for example, the increase in case referrals was extraordinary, sometimes reaching 100 per cent and more (*Community Care*, 20 February 1986, p. 2 and *Social Work Today*, 7 April 1986, p. 7). Along with this pressure has come a much tighter regulation of social work procedures so that more is prescribed and less is discretionary – hence the 'bureaucratisation' of child abuse in the strict sense of the word (Cooper, 1982).

Social services departments in particular, as the agency which carries ultimate legal responsibility for the protection of children, have been forced to take strong action because of public concern and, as we show, this is reflected in the statistics relating to children who come into their care.

Children in care

The main form of compulsory care of children is provided by *care orders* made under the Children and Young Persons Act 1969 in Juvenile Court hearings.

In England and Wales between 1977 and 1983, the number of children subject to such orders dropped from 45 800 to 39 900 (at 31 March). Within these overall figures juvenile offenders have declined (Section 7(7) of the Act) from 17 600 to 10 900, while ill-treated children (Section I 2(a)) have increased from 13 800 to 18 000 (DHSS, 1983).

Wardship is an ancient legal procedure by which the High Court can protect children. Until the second half of the 1970s, it was rarely used by, and even unknown to most local authority social workers. This has changed greatly as social services departments have increasingly sought new ways to achieve some control over children they consider at risk. Between 1971 and 1981 the number of applications for wardship rose from 622 to 1903 (Parton, 1985, p. 125).

Voluntary Care differs from Care Orders in that children come into care as the result of an agreement between their parents and social services departments (Section 2 Child Care Act 1980). Evidence is clear that the relationship between these two forms of care – voluntary and compulsory – has been changing steadily. Hence:

Year	1972	1977	1983
Voluntary Care	46	45.4	34.9
Care Orders	38.2	45.8	38.9

England at 31 March. Thousands.

Source: DHSS, 1983.

Within voluntary care, the same statistics record 'reasons' for admission and these have moved from what one might call the 'simple' end (mother's illness, death of parents) to the 'difficult' end (unsatisfactory home conditions). This suggests that previously social services departments and parents co-operated to deal with temporary family crisis, whereas now children come into care under more troubled and complex circumstances. Once in care, they tend to stay longer and are generally an older group.

Even where care begins voluntarily, it is possible for social services departments to change the arrangement by assuming (taking away) the rights of one or both parents of a child (Section 3 Child Care Act 1980) without recourse to the courts. This practice has grown steadily in the ten years until 1983 and again the reasons given are more likely to indicate parental failure rather than misfortune; while it may be one thing to take over the rights of a parent who is dead or who suffers from a 'permanent disability' or 'mental disorder', it is another to judge 'failure of obligations'. Again, the reason for assuming parental rights, introduced by the Children Act 1975, namely that the child had been in voluntary care continuously for three years, has been used readily by social services departments (Short Report, 1983, p. 33).

Place of Safety Orders are the most drastic and immediate means available to social workers to remove a child from serious danger. Applications are most commonly made by an individual worker to a single magistrate and although figures are not available, it is possible that they are rarely refused. Once in force, the child can be held for up to 28 days, there is no right of appeal and parents are not always told where their child has been placed. Reinforced by police powers of entry, the Place of Safety Order is a vital protection for children who need rescuing from danger. Where children are in hospital, they acquire immediate protection from parents who may try to remove them and thus deny them proper medical investigation and treatment.

Just as the numbers of Care Orders related to child abuse have risen, so have Place of Safety Orders. Analysis is complicated by the fact that the method of collecting statistics was altered after 1976. Thus for England and Wales:

Year	1973	1974	1975	1976	1977	1978	1979	1980	1981	1982	1983
Place of Safety Orders	214	353	596	759	5876	5471	5705	6613	6212	6551	5726

At 31 March. Number made through the year.

Source: DHSS (Children's Division).

What is noticeable is the large increase in the three years 1974–6, following the Maria Colwell Inquiry.

Later studies by the Dartington Social Research Unit

(1983) and by Packman *et al.* (1986) give greater information about social services departments' use of Place of Safety Orders. The Dartington study found that:

1. Place of Safety Orders frequently led to full compulsory care and only 9 per cent resulted in voluntary care.
2. 73 per cent of the sample remained in care for more than two years.
3. The orders were taken out not only as a response to actual incidents of abuse, but also for 'preventative and investigative reasons'.
4. There were considerable variations between social services departments as to the proportion of Place of Safety Orders within total numbers of children within care, ranging from 12 per cent to 30 per cent (Packman found figures of 27 per cent to 38 per cent).

Although children of all ages were studied, it is the young and physically vulnerable who form the majority. Most of them were already known to social services departments, which suggests a pattern of rising concern which culminates in a child's sudden removal from home. This can mean either that the protective services are working well by identifying children at risk early and taking strong action to avert a crisis; alternatively, it may mean that the kind of families that social services departments most often work with – at the bottom end of society – are now given much less margin for error in the care of these children. If children removed by Place of Safety Orders are already known to social services departments, this may also challenge the view held by some that serious child abuse occurs at all levels of society; if this were true, one would expect to see more 'unknown' children removed in this way.

Supervision orders

Not all child abuse is so serious that it requires children to be removed from home. As definitions have broadened to include emotional abuse and failure to thrive, one might expect that official supervision of children families would have grown. Supervision orders are available under the

Children and Young Persons Act 1969 on children from birth to 17 years, but there is no evidence that their use has increased at the same rate as other stronger forms of intervention. In common with care orders, their incidence rose through the 1970s until 1977 and thereafter declined.

Year	1972	1977	1983
Supervision Orders	7.9	17.7	14.4

England at 31 March. Thousands.

However there are important age differences for while those over 10 years (who include criminal offenders) have declined significantly, those under 10 years have risen slightly.

Year	1977	1983
Under 10 years	2.1	2.5
Over 10 years	15.6	11.1

England at 31 March. Thousands.

and both groups have shown a decline from 1980 to 1983 (Supervision Orders (England) 1983, DHSS).

There is some corroboration from the Dartington study which found that only 9 per cent of their sample of children had experienced Supervision Orders before Place of Safety Orders (Dartington, 1983, p. 12).

Our impression is that social services departments (or perhaps juvenile courts) have not considered Supervision Orders as very relevant to tackling child abuse; this contrasts with the juvenile police system where supervision, especially with Intermediate Treatment provisions, has attracted government funding and enthusiastic support from social workers. In fact about 90 per cent of Supervision Orders are made in criminal proceedings and of those made in care proceedings as many as 40 per cent may relate to non-school attendance rather than ill-treatment (DHSS, 1985, p. 6).

Supervision orders are made on children rather than on their parents and this may have seemed a major weakness where social workers need to exert some control over the way a child is being looked after at home. The DHSS Review of Child Care Law has considered this matter and recommended ways of strengthening the order: however, it is noticeable that the subject receives far less attention (only six pages) than the question of how children should be admitted to care and specific recommendations do not include clear sanctions against parents who do not co-operate (DHSS, 1985a, pp. 130–6).

Social Services Departments and abusing families

Annual statistics relating to children in care demonstrate that social services departments have become more concerned about children seen to be at risk and more ready to take strong action in whatever ways the law allows. Equally, courts concerned with divorce, custody, access and maintenance matters have increasingly committed children to care or placed them under the supervision of social services departments (Short Report, 1983, vol. I, p. LX). Where previously, voluntary agreements were common it is now more likely that parents will experience formally legally enforced relationships with social services departments, and negotiations are likely to be more contentious through adversarial disputes in court.

The law has moved away from an optimistic family support philosophy embodied in the Children and Young Persons Act 1963 to more explicit child protection at the expense of the parents as expressed by the Children Act 1975 which also gave important encouragement to foster parents and adopters. Coming into care and remaining there have attracted more attention than measures to provide preventive help to families. Even where parents' rights have been re-affirmed (as in 1983 legislation about access to their children in care) the future is unlikely to make the relationship between social services departments and parents any easier. If anything the Review of Child Care Law Report, in its otherwise commendable desire for justice, may be paving the way for proceedings in juvenile courts to become even more complex and daunting for parents than they are now.

The latest and most widely reported Inquiry into the death

of Jasmine Beckford (Beckford Report, 1985, esp. pp.293–5) developed a central criticism that local authority social workers were reluctant to carry out properly their parental role on behalf of children in care and tended to be over-optimistic about family rehabilitation. Whatever happened in that case, the overall picture does not support the criticism. Social services departments have shown themselves ready and willing to challenge the wishes of parents and to exclude them where necessary from the care of their children. It is perhaps a pity that sensational aspects of isolated cases seem to count more than solid national evidence.

At risk registers

In the absence of co-ordinated central government assessment of child abuse, local information is available through at risk registers which are the responsibility of Area Review Committees; these bodies were set up following DHSS recommendations in 1974, are multi-disciplinary and represent the main agencies who have a responsibility or interest in child abuse. In many cases they have utilised the resources of the NSPCC to organise and maintain such registers which can best be seen as a measure of official work done with children who may be at risk of abuse.

In 1976 DHSS felt obliged to issue another circular (DHSS, 1976a) because only 80 per cent of Area Review Committees had introduced registers. Later in the year (DHSS, 1976b) they also recommended the involvement of police in case conferences on child abuse and approved the release of information where appropriate, about adults' criminal convictions to welfare agencies. In the absence of clear central definitions it was inevitable that local registers would vary greatly in their criteria and use. Shearer's 1978 survey of social services departments, where there had previously been child abuse enquiries, reveals large variations in numbers, from 30 in one area to hundreds in others (Shearer, 1979, p. 14). DHSS were eventually compelled to issue another circular in 1980 which both specified and widened register categories; their list comprised physical injury, physical neglect, failure to thrive, emotional abuse, and children in the same household as others previously abused (DHSS, 1980). Although DHSS decided against including sexual abuse as a category, it has been adopted by many Area Review Committees, though with varying criteria we suspect.

At risk registers reflect concern rather than incidence of child abuse. As we indicated previously they are very sensitive to public alarms and their recorded figures, therefore, need cautious analysis. It would appear that central government's role in defining and monitoring the extent of abuse has been largely reactive; as a result, local views of abuse remain erratic and unsupported by an reliable framework. This is a serious weakness of registers for if they are over-inclusive they lose their value both to welfare workers and to statisticians.

The dilemma of intervention

Good child care must require a balanced approach by local authority social workers. While it is appropriate and understandable that voluntary agencies, researchers and theorists should pursue their own preferences, the state, both at central and local level, surely has a duty to act cautiously to evaluate findings about child abuse before shaping its policies and procedures. This has not been easy in a period of strong and occasionally intense public concern and the data suggest that social services departments have become much more ready to remove children from families or to resist their return. At the same time, central government has been reluctant to play its full role in analysing and consolidating the huge quantity of research, proposals and practices which have grown around child abuse.

Clearly social services departments have become much more protective towards children at risk but this is only in the immediate short-term sense. In the longer term the question arises whether children who enter care have a better life. A major DHSS summary in 1985 of nine research projects into child care decisions suggests that life for children in care can be threatened by poor planning, placement upheavals, changes in social worker, and the loss of links with natural families (DHSS, 1985c).

Regarding this particular matter of admitting children into care compulsorily, the report says: 'It is noteworthy that compulsion is against most social workers' ethos, although it is increasingly being used. The idea seems to be to "get control in order to plan and safeguard". Yet constructive planning seems all too often absent' (DHSS, 1985c, p. 19). It follows then, that children can sometimes be abused, in the wide sense, by the state as well as by their parents. In Chapter 4 we explore further this dilemma that social workers as helpers may themselves constitute a hazard to children's welfare – a further demonstration of the uniquely difficult role of social services departments in child abuse.

Summary

Child abuse has been characterised by growth since its 'discovery' in the 1960s: growth in public concern, in its definition, in professional activity and in the reaction of social workers in their role of agents of the state.

A constantly expanding definition of child abuse has posed serious problems, both moral and practical, for all workers involved in the field and seems to have produced more confrontation with parents than can be explained simply on the basis of statistics about child injury and death. It is right that social services departments, in particular, should be sensitive to public opinion. However, because of the power they may hold over the lives of children and their families it is crucial that they act with caution and a proper sense of perspective. This is difficult because we still lack centrally collated and co-ordinated information or research about exactly what is child abuse. It therefore follows that if definition is difficult, the right kind and level of prevention and protection by social services departments is not easily discovered and there are not likely to be any simple exclusive solutions.

2

Other Agencies and Child Abuse

Child abuse, by its nature, is not the province of any one group of workers. The public alarms about children have reverberated, to a greater or lesser degree, through all the workers and agencies who have contact with children; they have been forced to communicate and collaborate and official enquiries have regularly complained where they have apparently failed to do so. It is probably true to say that the central theme of official reports has been liaison between workers rather than the efficacy of particular methods of treatment of child abuse. If only workers were quicker to share concerns, it would seem then perhaps most children would not have died.

Inter-disciplinary collaboration is desirable in any field of social work and this chapter will therefore review the features of the main workers and agencies with whom local authority social workers liaise. The welfare services are far from homogeneous and it is thus important to have some understanding of their attitudes, philosophies and practice.

Doctors

This umbrella term covers seven main groups of workers: paediatricians, obstetricians and gynaecologists, general hospital doctors, general practitioners, psychiatrists, community medicine specialists and police surgeons. All these groups with the exception of the general hospital doctors gave evidence to the Parliamentary Select Committee on Violence in the family (1976–7 session) and their contributions reflect often widely differing viewpoints.

19

Paediatricians

This group has the closest association with child abuse, having published, as far back as 1966, guidelines for the management of the condition. Their evidence to the Select Committee is detailed and forceful (vol. II, pp. 140–5) going far beyond basic medical issues and into the realms of inter-disciplinary and legal matters. Well before this time paediatricians, especially through the Tunbridge Wells Group, had probably exerted considerable influence as Parton (1985, ch. 4) argues both on the government's reaction to the Maria Colwell enquiry and on the subsequent Children Act 1975.

Paediatricians are important to social workers for several reasons: firstly, they make the key medical diagnosis on children referred to them which determine whether removal from home is necessary; secondly, the paediatrician's secure status in the field is important in securing the support of other workers, especially general practitioners; thirdly, their role as expert witnesses is a factor in bringing cases before the juvenile court. As their name suggests, paediatricians' direct concern is with children as patients, an approach which may be useful in counterbalancing the social workers' broader view of the family context. It is clear when we consider attitudes during the 1970s and 1980s that the viewpoint of 'child first, family second' has become dominant. The Children Act 1975 endorsed and encouraged work to protect children, reduced the prospects of rehabilitation of abused children and smoothed the path towards long-term fostering and adoption. Earlier intervention, more vigorous removal from home and wider definitions of abuse have characterised paediatricians' views of child abuse. Along with these has been substantial research in the field by this group of workers.

Obstetricians and gynaecologists

Pregnancy circumstances are acknowledged to be important indicators of child and family health. A woman who does not want her baby, neglects herself during pregnancy, has an inadequate diet, suffers a difficult birth, is unsupported by family and friends or who finds it difficult to bond with her baby, is giving important warning signs. Research by Lynch and Roberts (1977) has indicated that much useful information exists about mothers in maternity hospitals although it is not always understood or passed on.

Many such factors become the province of doctors concerned with pregnancy and birth in hospitals yet they are a group who may not have regular liaison with social workers. It may be significant that most of the official enquiries into child deaths concern themselves inevitably with periods of months leading up to the deaths; it might be more instructive if their investigations extended further back in time to prenatal events. If so, it is important to consider the relationship between obstetricians and gynaecologists and social workers. Where children's hospitals are close geographically to maternity hospitals it seems likely that social workers will forge a more active, preventive liaison. An example of this is in Bristol where the Royal Hospital for Sick Children is only yards from the Maternity Hospital. The social workers who are closely involved in child abuse cases receive frequent referrals from the maternity section and are able to make contact with mothers at risk at an earlier stage. Elsewhere it is more likely that hospital social workers may be based in a general hospital setting, spend much of their time with elderly clients and have far less active links with maternity hospitals.

Amongst the welter of research, often contradictory, about indicators of child abuse, health, pregnancy and the experience of childbirth are often cited. The evidence submitted to the Select Committee reveals a range of views about mothers in hospital: it touches on cultural and intelligence factors, housing and economic difficulties, the value of natural childbirth, medical technology, hospital practices and many other issues which together can provide a picture that might make sense to an enquiring social worker (vol. II, pp. 306–22).

Although these are issues for all social workers, they are particularly relevant for those based in hospitals. Thus gynaecologists run regular clinics which bring to light a wide range of patients' problems from abortion to marital and sexual difficulties.

It is also worth remembering that other parts of the health

service have a key role in maternity and childhood. In addition to health visitors, who will be discussed later, midwives and school nurses are in a position both to look for signs of trouble and to offer advice to young parents. The social worker should not neglect these staff when building up local information networks, and the DHSS draft guidelines on child abuse issued in 1986 stress the importance of the health authority role (DHSS, 1986a esp. pp. 4–5).

Hospital doctors

To the extent that many children who suffer injuries are taken to hospital, the response they receive there is an important link in the chain of child abuse detection. Although guidelines are issued to accident and emergency departments to encourage alertness, social workers should not assume that an expert service (in child abuse terms) is always available.

A small study by Dingwall *et al.* (1983, pp. 37–47) suggests that several factors may militate against efficient detection of child abuse in the hospital. Firstly the majority of patients in the accident and emergency department are children anyway, many of whom suffer from genuine accidents. Thus child abuse awareness may become dulled. Secondly, a kind of organisational and medico-professional 'framing' may predispose the doctor (a Senior House Officer) towards thinking that parents are unlikely to injure their children. Thirdly, Senior House Officers are 'in transit', often doing the accident and emergency work for only six months as part of their training. The work does not have high status and more exotic forms of illness may have a greater appeal to the doctor. He may also be young and even a student from abroad which itself may cause language difficulties and perhaps a different cultural view of child-rearing.

It follows that while paediatricians can be expected to be alert to the possibility of child abuse, this is less likely in the accident and emergency department. For social workers there are two issues: the field social worker who may attend hospital to follow up an allegation, needs to express concerns skilfully yet forcefully to medical staff; this may involve demanding second opinions from paediatricians where necessary; for hospital social workers, the need is to develop their status and role within hospitals by personal contacts, circulating papers, statistics and by promoting and seeking joint training opportunities.

General practitioners

As a group, general practitioners are the most important medical figures for social workers in child abuse. The DHSS Review of Inquiries shows in its Appendix that general practitioners were involved in 17 out of the 18 cases studied (DHSS, 1981, app. I). Long before they ever arrive at the hospital, most children will have been seen in local surgeries with general or specific ailments.

Of all medical groups, we suspect that general practitioners can arouse the most frustration in social workers. They are an essential part of family life, yet in terms of teamwork they may be the most elusive. They have been criticised certainly as often as social workers following child deaths yet as a group they appear to have made few major changes in their methods of dealing with children and families.

Hallett and Stevenson (1980, pp. 36–8) have considered the role of GPs in terms of their familiarity with child abuse, how often they refer cases to social workers and their attitudes towards case conferences. The first point to make is that GPs are generalists not specialists and this is borne out by the tone of the evidence of the Royal College of General Practitioners to the Select Committee (vol. II, pp. 148–57). While concern is expressed and general exhortations are made, there is a lack of really informed argument or any radical suggestions for changing the way GPs work with children and families who may raise concern. Similarly, the BMAs *Handbook of Medical Ethics* contains no specific reference to 'child abuse', 'non-accidental injury' or 'battered children' (British Medical Association, 1981).

The relationship between GPs and social workers is not simple. As well as possible cultural differences, the two forms of training often have dissimilar emphasis; the medical model stresses concise diagnosis leading to specific treatments, the almost sacred importance of individual responsibility and a rather hierarchical hospital-based view of teamwork. Social work on the other hand is more concerned with eclectic, multi-disciplinary approaches, flexibility, client participation, teamwork and conformity within organisations. It is not surprising then if the two groups, one professional and the other semi-professional by public estimation, do not always collaborate. Significantly the BMA handbook, while supporting inter-disciplinary work says: 'Social workers, like some other groups, have evolved no effective sanctions to safeguard confidentiality and there is currently no compulsion on social workers to register with a disciplinary body' (British Medical Association, 1981, p. 46).

Thus the general medical view, and one that presumably reflects the perceptions of many GPs, is that there are some risks attached to referring cases to social workers. The growing trend to allow access by local authority councillors to social services case files may aggravate this situation and at the BMA's 1983 Annual Representative Meeting the following resolution was passed: 'That in view of the Law Lords' ruling, which allows access by local authority members to medical records held by their social services and other departments, doctors in clinical practice be advised to withhold medical information unless confidentiality can be assured'.

Such suspicions may affect the GP's attitude towards case conferences as one part of a process which once started can 'appear to have the momentum of a fully laden super-tanker' (Weir, 1983, p. 16). A study in Devon Social Services of child abuse case conferences over a six-month period in 1978 put GP attendances at 18 per cent compared with 86 per cent for Area Health Authority Staff, 90 per cent for health visitors and 44 per cent for Police (Devon Social Services Dept., 1978). GPs may have various reasons for such levels of attendance and because they are important to such conferences, social workers need to consider what these might be.

If GPs say they are 'too busy' to attend, this may reflect a general feature of the GP system within our society which is unlikely to change. If, however, GPs lack knowledge of child abuse and its consequences it is important for social workers to communicate such information by follow-up letters, details of court hearings, subject to confidentiality. More importantly they may need to reduce the GP's suspicion that social workers lack individual responsibility for their cases and are merely agents of bureaucracies. In our view, relationships grow in time and the trend in recent years for social workers to remain longer in post will help. Further, as the GP is a generalist we are inclined to think a social worker who occupies a similar local role, through a patch system arrangement, is in a good position to collaborate enough with the GP to achieve some acceptance. Specialist (child care) roles may convince the GP that the social worker has particular skills but their contacts may also be infrequent. Child abuse detection and prevention ultimately depend more on frequent low-level communication than on occasional formal consultations.

We may have painted a gloomy view of the role of GPs in child abuse. This is particularly because we are struck by their generally muted reaction to public concerns in contrast to the massive soul-searching within social work. It might be the case that while one group has done too much, the other has done too little. The aim now should be to achieve a mid-point arrived at through developing trust between the two local services. The importance of the GPs to social workers is their secure local base within the community, their regular contact with wide sections of the population and thus their sense of perspective about the people they treat.

Psychiatrists

The relationship between psychiatrists and social workers benefits from the fact that both groups at times draw on similar areas of knowledge, less precise than is the case with most other medical workers. The continuing movement towards community care has involved psychiatrists in multidisciplinary teamwork in which the social worker is an important figure. In addition, the role of the social worker in psychiatric hospital admissions and discharges again promotes co-operation.

Psychiatrists have often seen child abuse as a major challenge, especially in the search to seek specific psycho-pathologies of abusers. As recipients of referrals from GPs they may well become involved in a parental breakdown that leads eventually to an inquiry to a child. Child psychiatrists will offer help in situations where a child is presented as the cause or the symptom of family strife and the growth of family therapy techniques has encouraged a wider view of the problem.

Despite the apparent importance of psychiatrists in child abuse they may not, in fact, be involved very frequently. The DHSS Review of Inquiries shows their involvement in only four out the eighteen cases recorded. We can perhaps connect this to the lack of consensus about the psychopathology of abusers; despite considerable research there is no solid evidence that people who ill-treat their children even seri-ously are likely to suffer from clinical mental illness (Borland, 1976; Baker *et al.*, 1976). Despite long term research, Oliver, in his latest detailed study of 147 abusing families (Oliver, 1983) is hard put to produce any distinct set of abuser characteristics that easily lend themselves to specific psychi-atric treatments.

Psychiatrists' relationships with social workers have also been influenced by reorganisation in SSDs.

The move towards specialisation demonstrated by the creation of Approved Social Workers in Mental Health may have two effects: while it will eventually offer psychiatrists a more expert service in the field of adults' problems it will also reduce contact with generic social workers or those who are concerned mainly with children. However as psychiatric hospitals close or reduce their function, community care for the mentally ill offers opportunities for such workers to set up contacts with psychiatrists in local settings.

There is a potentially valuable relationship between psychiatrists, general practitioners and social workers if teamwork is accepted and developed. For the social worker, the psychiatrist can offer skills as a therapist either to the parents or the whole family and is also a source of expertise about the nature of mental illness and the effects and side-effects of drug and other treatments.

Community physicians (child health)

This group of staff, formerly known as medical officers, are employed by health authorities and have a wide-ranging role to promote and monitor the health of children. Their preventative and educational work in clinics and schools gives them a useful socio-medical viewpoint and the nature of their work involves frequent inter-disciplinary discussion.

The under fives are at most risk of child abuse and community physicians often develop links with nurseries and playgroups where their informal, advisory role can support staffs dealing with children. For older children the school may often be the place where injuries and ill-health are first noticed and the community physicians can help teachers distinguish between serious and trivial incidents. As with GPs, they have a knowledge of socio-medical norms and thus deviations in local populations; context is important in diagnosing child abuse and the experienced community physician will have some understanding of school catchment areas and their characteristics. The value of this kind of knowledge is that it can act as a filter for referrals to social workers.

In particular cases the community physicians may not play a major role. Occasionally they may be asked to examine children where the GP is unwilling or unable, but this may present them with difficult ethical, even legal dilemmas. Now that social workers may have the power to insist on medical examinations of children subject to supervision orders made in care proceedings, this situation is more likely to arise if a GP is reluctant to jeopardise a relationship with a family.

Community physicians can also play valuable roles both as members of Area Review Committees and as mediators between social workers and other medical workers. In some areas they chair child abuse case conferences and we find this appropriate; they are detached from the family, they may well be able to coax reluctant GPs to attend meetings and they are free from the preoccupations about what legal action to take which must influence an SSD chairman. Nevertheless, for a social worker the community physician (child health) may remain a remote figure, unless the two workers collaborate and share local knowledge.

Police surgeons

Such doctors will often be GPs who are contracted to the police in matters or criminal injury. Their evidence to the Select Committee makes interesting reading (vol. III, pp. 586–9). Essentially, although they may not feature often in child abuse cases, they appeared to welcome more involvement in three ways: firstly, to act as liaison officers between various agencies, secondly, by applying their general experience of suspicious injuries to the examination of children, and thirdly, through their knowledge of medical jurisprudence, to present evidence in court with (they imply) greater confidence and expertise than some of their medical colleagues. Certainly Care Proceedings court cases are adversorial occasions which may involve separate counsel for the child, the parents and the SSD and thus prove an ordeal even for 'expert' witnesses.

There has been a general tendency in England and Wales for the law and child abuse to become closely linked even if parents themselves are rarely prosecuted. SSDs have sought Care Orders more frequently in the past ten years and there may be occasions when the police surgeon's ability to relate child abuse to wider views of criminal injury can be valuable to courts. Finally, we should point out that forensic pathologists have at times played an important part in influencing attitudes towards child abuse.

Health visitors

Health visitors are involved in child care abuse cases as frequently as GPs and social workers because of their general role in visiting young families. Inevitably they have attracted their share of criticism in official enquiries and this has provoked almost as much self-analysis of their work as we find among social workers. Such reviews reveal interesting and distinctive dilemmas for health visiting and highlight two main issues.

Firstly, the overall aim of health visiting is to be considered. Is it to offer a general preventative monitoring educational and advisory service to as many young families as possible or is it to devote disproportionate amounts of time to a few families where child abuse is suspected or identified? The second problem concerns the professional and legal implications of actually working closely with abusing families. Both issues have been explored elsewhere (see Parton, 1985, ch. 3; Hallett and Stevenson, 1980, pp. 27–31; Select Committee, vol. II, pp. 97–112) and the Health Visitors' Association (HVA) has issued policy statements on the matter of the 'key worker' in child abuse cases. This term was introduced by a DHSS 1976 Circular (1976a, para. 29 p. v) to denote the worker who would co-ordinate and manage the actual work with the children and families. Although SSD social workers normally occupy this role conferred on them by Case Conference decisions, in some cases health visitors have taken on the duties.

Key worker or prime worker?

The HVA General Secretary in an open letter to Area Health Authorities dated 15 July 1981 expressed the Association's alarm and exasperation following criticisms of some of its members in official enquiries:

> My committee believes that a Health Visitor in touch with a family at risk, should continue to provide health visiting services and should liaise promptly and regularly with the appointed 'Key Worker', but that if she agrees to take on the extra duties of 'Key Worker' herself she will inevitably be failing to visit other families who might, with her help, be prevented from reaching a similar stage of breakdown.

Subsequently in 1982 the HVA issued a joint statement first with BASW (*Social Work Today*, 25 January 1983) and soon after with the Nursing and Midwifery Professions (Joint Report, 1982) which proposed a distinction between the 'Key Worker' who has statutory case management responsibilities and the 'Prime Worker' who may undertake most of the work with a family.

Is this merely playing with words? Are health visitors trying to write themselves out of the minefield of child abuse accountability? We do not believe this and welcome what seems to be a sensible attempt by the HVA to clarify what is often a very muddled and worrying situation for all workers. Clearly health visitors do not have the same statutory responsibilities as social workers and it is important that definitions of their role do not confuse this issue. Secondly, there is no reason to believe that health visitors are opting out of child abuse work. A training paper by Sharman, Professional Advisor to the Council for the Education and Training of Health Visitors (CCETHV) is emphatic about the need for vigorous work with families at risk, more child abuse content in basic and post-qualifying training courses, inter-disciplinary induction courses and the possibilities for team-work (Sharman, undated).

Benefits of a separate role

Child abuse concerns have produced a widespread tightening of statutory roles and duties and ultimate legal accountability is clearly defined as the province of the local authority social worker. We see no extra benefit in shackling health visitors with apparently similar responsibilities and the anxiety that goes with them. There is also a risk of confusing clients still further if the same role is shared by workers from quite different settings who have different parts to play in child abuse. To define a health visitor as a 'Key Worker' is to impose a form of accountability which is misleading and unhelpful given the constitution of health visiting.

The health visitor faces more than enough dilemmas in deciding how to work with families at risk, yet can offer valuable distinctive help that may complement and even compensate for what the social worker is doing. Firstly, she has knowledge of child development norms and thus deviations; secondly she has a well understood public role in visiting families which can enable access more easily than for the social worker; thirdly, she has an important two-way relationship with the GP, both for encouraging medical examinations and also for teasing out and directing medical information towards the social worker; fourthly, her skills in counselling, advising and educating parents can complement but not duplicate social work activity. In many child abuse cases treatment will be required in differing ways and at different levels; thus a mother with serious marital problems may simultaneously need encouragement to improve basic maternal skills and information to understand how her baby behaves.

In summary we welcome the stance of HVA in resisting the imposition of the 'Key Worker' role. Like social workers, health visitors occupy a semi-professional position in society. The two groups have had to bend in the force of the strong winds that have blown across the child abuse scene; if health visitors are now digging their heels they are merely making the important point that good work in child abuse does not necessarily require new job descriptions. They are also, indirectly, reminding social workers and others of one important fact, namely that health visitors have no legal power of entry to the homes of children. They can only work with families by consent.

The police

Within two years of the major DHSS circular (1974b) which defined the ground rules for child abuse policy they were obliged to issue another one 1976 (1976b) to provide recommendations and guidelines to cover the role of the police. To the extent that child abuse is a crime in which the police are likely to be involved then some government statement was clearly needed because of general uncertainty about how, when and even why the police should enter into investigations and discussions. As a result there have been important changes and in this section we shall concentrate on three main questions: firstly, the police role in child abuse investigation; secondly, in subsequent case planning, and thirdly, as far as general philosophical considerations are concerned.

The growth of police involvement

As we showed in Chapter 1, with reference to criminal statistics, the number of parents and caretakers who are actually prosecuted for offences against children, is small. Such cases therefore occupy a minute part of overall police criminal investigation and have to compete with preoccupations about theft and mugging, as well as terrorism and industrial disputes.

However, once general concerns about all forms of child abuse escalated in 1974 so the involvement of the police grew correspondingly. If the early approach was based on a disease model it was complicated because, by definition, if child abuse was suspected, investigated and identified the question of legal offence arose. Social work and medical staff were to some extent hoist with their own petard, for the more vigorously and publicly they pursued child abuse the more likely it was they would attract police attention. Early suspicions of the police gave way to an acceptance, grudging often, that a dialogue was necessary.

As a result of the 1976 circular, the police became regular attenders at case conferences. More importantly, they were encouraged by the DHSS to make available relevant criminal records and other information about parents and caretakers that might assist in investigations of child abuse; this stemmed particularly from the Maria Colwell (DHSS, 1974a) and Richard Auckland (DHSS, 1975) cases where men with previous convictions were the attackers. The police and local authority social workers have much in common as well as major differences. Both groups are very sensitive to public and government opinion, both work within large formal organisations and, most importantly, they share the onerous role of both investigator and prosecutor. Thus the police response to child abuse was to extend and specify their procedures and guidelines about liaison with other agencies. Designated senior officers often attended all case conferences within given areas and developed good working relationships, particularly with social services staff. Police training expanded to take account of child abuse and in certain police forces the topic acquired more status. In Devon, for example, a detective chief superintendent is heavily involved in child abuse work, has been one of the key authors of the County booklet (Devon Review Committee, 1984), attends international conferences and has regular contacts with leading paediatricians and psychiatrists. Northampton is another force whose policies towards child abuse have been energetic and collaborative.

Investigations

Once the police became involved in case conferences a next step was collaboration with social workers in the investigation itself. Social workers lack the training, and perhaps the inclination, to interrogate parents and caretakers who are under suspicion. Where the police have offered some reassurance that they can acknowledge the particularly complex and painful nature of child abuse they have often investigated effectively. Joint training courses between police and social workers have helped the groups to move towards each other, the social workers in accepting that they must seek accurate information about incidents and the police in understanding more about family dynamics and tensions and in appreciating the treatment possibilities that lie beyond the discovery of abuse.

One of the consequences of police and social services collaboration was to bring an increase in general alertness. Police officers are often called to investigate domestic incidents and in such cases they may even act as an unofficial and very useful arm of SSD emergency services. It is now more likely that the condition and circumstances of children in such situations will be noticed and reported on. However, individual police officers may find their discretion now more restricted as was the case when consultation with social workers became normal police policy under the Children and Young Persons Act 1969.

Child abuse investigation with its criminal as well as helping elements has made co-operation between police and social workers inevitable. Useful dialogues now exist and it seems in general that the two services recognise the need to co-operate in the investigation process. Women police officers can often play a valuable role, visiting either on their own or jointly with social workers. In our view parents have a right to know that they are being investigated and social workers have sometimes been guilty of concealing their intentions under the guise of 'popping in to see how the children are getting on'.

Case management

Once child abuse has been discovered in a family the police still have a part to play. The 1976 DHSS circular (DHSS, 1976b) acknowledged the difficulties but urged police authorities to be flexible about prosecuting parents and caretakers and to take account of the overall needs of the child and any other plans regarding the family. It is not possible from criminal statistics to isolate general assaults within families on children but our impression is that the police have generally responded to the DHSS advice. In fact, where they may wish to prosecute parents against the wishes of other agencies it is normal police practice for the matter to be referred to the Chief Constable and even beyond to the Director of Public Prosecutions and for the reasons to be set out in writing.

Timing of the prosecution of parents, the effects on the child and overall police invovement with the family are all important issues in case management which can be and usually are discussed fully at case conferences. It will sometimes be possible to orchestrate police procedures to minimise the trauma for the child. Parents are almost ceratin to see the police as menacing figures, but this can be utilised if it allows the social worker and other workers to develop their helping role through an agreed division of tasks. Information available to police can also be incorporated in monitoring children who remain at home. Parents under stress are often those who commit other criminal offences and the transfer and interpretation of such information may help to build up a warning picture to social workers.

Philosophical considerations

A major effect of the official concern about child abuse has been to encourage collaboration between powerful state agencies and professionals. Without caution, principles and a proper sense of perspective, that collaboration can come to look more like conspiracy. This is a particular danger where the police are involved because theirs' is essentially a criminal view of the world. At risk registers which are too wide and speculative in their categories can simply serve to bring more individuals to the notice of the police through case conferences. Worse, those individuals may not even be aware that they have been registered. A survey in 1983 revealed that 22 out of 38 responding SSDs did not always inform parents and 28 out of 37 said they would object to parents being able to check the accuracy of register records (*Community Care*, 12 May 1983, pp. 17–19). The very co-operation we have otherwise approved can easily lead to familiarity that breeds contempt for privacy; 'relevant' information about parents may encompass the swapping of almost any snippets of knowledge. The 1976 DHSS circular also encouraged its own staffs in supplementary benefits offices to respond to requests from SSDs about transient families and this poses similar risks to individual freedoms.

The social worker needs to maintain a fine balance in dealing with the police. Honest co-operation for specific reasons in certain cases is necessary and desirable, particularly where adult caretakers have serious criminal records of assault, child molesting, and so on. Beyond that the social worker must always ask himself or herself, 'What do I need to know? What is relevant and what is *irrelevant* to my enquiries? Are exchanges of information becoming just an unthinkable routine? When do I keep things to myself? How does child abuse affect my normal rules of confidentiality?'

National Society for the Prevention of Cruelty to Children

We end this chapter by looking at an agency which, for many, epitomises work in the child abuse field. In a short section we cannot do justice to a society which has celebrated (if that is the word) one hundred years of protecting children, instead we confine ourselves to a brief historical review before discussing the main trends and features of current NSPCC work. We make use of the three major headings set out in the

1983 NSPCC centenary chapter: 'Protection, Prevention and Pioneering' (NSPCC, 1983).

Protection

The rescue of children from terrible conditions is probably the most durable of images that the public has of the NSPCC. It has long had the power, unique in a voluntary society, to intervene, remove children and, if necessary, bring them before a juvenile court in their own interests (133 cases in 1983). Traditionally this work was carried out by uniformed inspectors who may often have been policemen themselves in previous careers. The 'cruelty man' remained a distinctive figure until the late 1960s when perhaps two factors changed the society's policy. The first was the growing professionalisation of social work in children's departments with their relatively high levels of trained staff. At that time the inspectors' status was declining and the uniform had come to represent a rather out-dated, simplistic and narrow approach to child care problems. The second influence was the deep impression made by the American 'discovery' (Pfohl, 1980, pp. 323–40) of child abuse on English, especially NSPCC, researchers and practitioners.

The inspectorate has survived these impacts, but the uniforms are gone, the workers are better trained and their approach more varied and sophisticated. Otherwise their central task, to intervene quickly and directly where children are at risk, seems to find continued approval from the public whose donations make up 80 per cent of the NSPCC's income. However, the inspectors have probably lost some ground in relation to the other arms of the service which we shall now consider.

Prevention

As the child abuse field has expanded, the urge to find solutions to the problem has also grown and the NSPCC has been at the centre of developments. The retrospective study of seventy-eight battered children known to inspectors in 1969 (Skinner and Castle, 1969) and the setting up of the

Denver House Unit in London in 1968 had more ambitious aims than merely child protection (Baker, Hyman *et al.*, 1976). In common with the general trends of research at that time the emphasis was firstly on long-term treatment of abusing families and secondly on seeking pre-disposing factors which, once identified, might help in preventing future abuse. These twin aims – research and treatment – formed the basis of the NSPCC's work through the 1970s.

The Denver House model did not set a rigid pattern. What is in fact striking is the variety of styles, methods and settings which have characterised the society's special units which now number thirteen in various parts of the country. For example, the Rochdale Unit has a particular focus on Family Therapy (Dale *et al.*, 1983), Barnsley has experimented with regular reviews of children at risk by 'standing' work groups (Fry, 1981, pp. 159–65) and the more recent unit in Plymouth, Devon, devoted much of the initial time to organising and chairing case conferences and reviews on behalf of the local statutory social services (R. Marriott, 1984). In other settings the Society has experimented with 24-hour telephone life-lines, parents' groups, day nurseries and playgroups, drop-in centres and preparation for parenthood schemes, as well as a variety of collaborative and consultative schemes with other agencies.

It is interesting to find such a variety in the NSPCC's work. Does it imply that the long-pursued 'disease model' with its implication of specific causes and specific remedies is not in the end, very productive? Alternatively, the Society's work can be seen as opportunist in the sense that the approach of any particular unit may depend on local circumstances, staff interests and joint-funding arrangements with other agencies, especially SSDs. For example, while the Coventry Unit, as reported in its Annual Review for 1982–3 (Coventry, NSPCC, 1983), shows a broad spread of work amongst its 'four offices', 200 referrals and 96 cases taken on for further investigation and support, the Plymouth unit is very different. Arising from a joint-funding arrangement with Devon SSD all its referrals are required to pass by way of local social work managers. At the time of enquiry the small unit had only 7 active cases. On the other hand the staff had been involved in over 300 case confereces and reviews in 1983, organised the at risk register for West Devon, and clearly had an important role in monitoring the formal and administrative aspects of the response to child abuse.

Pioneering

Apart from its direct work with clients, the Society has been very active in educational, advisory and lobbying work. Its extensive library, research literature and specialist staffing has been used to provide seminars and training courses for staff from other agencies. At a time in the early and middle 1970s when traditional specialisms had given way to the generic mode of SSDs, the NSPCC provided an important focus on expertise. The Society has also been active in pressing for changes in the law and for increased funds for child abuse work. Despite the recession it has survived, although it reported a revenue deficit that reached £2.1 million between 1979 and 1982 (NSPCC, 1982). Since that time, perhaps because of renewed public concern about child abuse, the Society has expanded its work with a current annual expenditure of approximately £11 million.

The NSPCC's future depends on the extent to which it can persuade the public and, to a lesser extent, government and local authorities, that it has something special to offer, something which can make a tangible impact on child abuse. What then can social workers expect from the NSPCC in the future?

The Society's Centenary Charter described a scheme to combine its staff into what it calls Child Protection Teams which would integrate the three arms of the services – Inspectors, Special Units and Day-Care facilities. The function of the new teams was to be:

1. direct casework with families
2. therapeutic and remedial services to the child
3. practical help in home management
4. day-care facilities for groups of children and parents
5. consultative and advisory services to the professions

6. instruction for schools, teachers, young people in preparation for parenthood
7. information through publicity and research to the professions and general public.

It is useful to see the Society's aims set out in such detail and the integration proposed would seem sensible in an organisation which has experienced a period of expansion and diversification. However, it is not clear how the different services and activities will interweave in practice and where one will take priority over another. Will the inspectorate increase or decline in relation to other staff? Will the emphasis be on intensive treatment, long or short term, with identified abusing families or will a greater investment be made in the long-term preventive services like preparation for parenthood?

A distinctive role

What seems clear is that the NSPCC has not been able to identify a particular method dealing with child abuse. Its plans suggest a multiple approach to a multi-causal problem. As such there is a danger for the Society that it may spread itself too thinly into areas of work already covered by other agencies. For example, community social work is advocated by the Barclay Committee (Barclay, 1982, ch. 13) as an important direction for SSDs; some of the NSPCCs targets are certainly within this area. It will be important therefore that NSPCC work in whatever mode bears a distinctive imprint that distinguishes it from more general social work activities.

As Parton has shown (Parton, 1985, ch. 3) the NSPCC was a central influence on child abuse thinking during the middle 1970s. Since then SSDs have stabilised despite, or perhaps because of, the economic recession. Their front-line staff are now more experienced and better qualified and there is now a significant movement back towards client-group specialisms in many SSDs. An effect may be to reduce the advantage the NSPCC enjoyed during the 1970s, when to an important extent, it represented a child care beacon. In our own view the Society could well face serious problems if it hopes to maintain its present level of expenditure and service.

Supporting or investigating

A possibility is for the NSPCC to reduce its inspectorate and to develop exclusively as a *helping* service. Its legal, protective functions merely duplicate the duties of SSDs and the conflicts between the role of authority and help may only confuse families. The massive anxiety about incidents of abuse has by now produced, indirectly, a countrywide system of registers, case conferences and investigation procedures that are as effective as human invention can achieve. The opportunity now exists for the NSPCC to use its considerable history, traditions and expertise to develop a comprehensive service that will complement the work of local authority social services departments. The main areas of activity might be as follows:

- research and data monitoring
- use of treatment methods related to specific population characteristics
- preparation for parenthood at school and beyond
- monitoring of legal aspects of child abuse
- provision of educational materials, training opportunities and consultancy
- specific community prevention programmes.

In our view the NSPCC stands at a difficult point in its history. After almost 20 years of hectic activity in the child abuse field the Society reflects a number of unresolved, competing issues. Local authority social workers face major difficulties in their own organisations and will need to turn to an alternative or complementary source of skill and knowledge. A sensibly structured NSPCC could provide this.

Summary

In this chapter we have attempted to trace the main features and activities of other workers in the child abuse field. Most of them have responded significantly to social and government pressures, and learned, sometimes reluctantly, to co-operate with each other more than before. Nevertheless, the important lesson for social workers is that such co-operation is defined by other workers' own values and agency policies and these vary considerably, hence the different reactions of health visitors and GPs. A proper appreciation of these differences is essential to teamwork in child abuse.

Perhaps a second lesson is that inter-disciplinary co-operation and communication does not itself solve the problem of child abuse. As we discussed earlier, the major recommendation of most official enquiries has been that various individuals and agencies should improve their liaison. In general this has been achieved by detailed procedures and guidelines for abuse cases. Nevertheless, it seems to us that the reasons why caretakers abuse their children are so complex that it may be dangerous for social workers to be too reassured by good relationships with other workers. Equally important is that individual workers should develop skills and resources distinctive to their particular roles. Where roles overlap too much – because everyone feels compelled to expand their activities – workers' own sense of responsibility and their capacity to operate independently with confidence may well be reduced.

Our impression is that after a period of almost frenzied co-operation, collaboration and communication, a number of agencies may need to withdraw somewhat to re-assess their various positions and re-state their differences.

The 1986 DHSS draft guidelines appear to acknowledge this and for the first time are a comprehensive attempt by central government to address themselves to all agencies who collaborate in child abuse work (DHSS, 1986a). This is of particular value to SSDs.

3

Social Workers' Anxieties and Needs

Although child abuse creates anxieties for all workers it is local authority social workers who must feel the greatest pressure. Not only do they carry legal responsibility, both short and long term, for the children they investigate but they have also increasingly borne the brunt of hostile and unsympathetic media and a society which is confused about the kind of service it wants for its children. Anxiety, then, is the constant companion of the local authority social worker. The 1978 DHSS study noted this in social worker responses which conveyed a strong sense of *individual* worry about cases (Parsloe *et al.*, 1978, p. 322).

SSD structure and anxiety

We have shown that SSDs have reacted strongly to child abuse pressures. The major effect has been a tightening up of procedures and structures in order to programme and standardise work. The booklets produced by most local authorities set out step-by-step guidelines in the belief that this will reduce risk to children and increase security for workers. Is this feasible?

Kakabadse (1982) sets out a useful framework for considering different kinds of SSD structures or 'cultures' as he calls them. The Role Culture lays strong emphasis on rules, roles and procedures with well-defined relationships between staff, while the Task Culture is more concerned with patterns to be defined by the task in hand, with flexibility and fluidity of roles. To date it would appear that SSDs have reacted to child abuse more in terms of a Role Culture than a Task Culture in that they have reduced flexibility and the professional discretion that accompanies it. Hallett and Stevenson (1980, pp. 12–18) raise similar concerns and discern a tendency for SSDs to play safe when under pressure.

As we urged in Chapter 1, it is vital that a state agency avoids extremes in its responses to a social problem; this is not only for the sake of children and families but also for its own workers. A preoccupation with tightening up procedures may in fact *increase* worker anxiety for two reasons: firstly because frontline staff become fearful that they will slip up and deviate from the procedures and secondly because the child abuse investigation cannot ultimately be done 'according to the book'. Hence there is a dissonance between ends and means. Parsloe, in seeking a balance between extremes suggests that:

> Clients require the skilled judgement based on professional responsibility which allows action to be taken in individual circumstances where no rules exist and where innovation may be required. But they also need the protection of rules which establish a basic minimum standard of service and ethical behaviour (Parsloe, 1981, p. 134).

Patch versus specialist structures

Child abuse work may be conducted in two broad ways within SSDs: either through specialist child care teams or through generic teams which are responsible for small local areas. The latter are known as 'patch' teams and have been discussed broadly within the Barclay Report (1982, app. A) and by Hadley and Hatch (1981) and Hadley and McGrath (1980, 1984).

It is not possible here to give a detailed analysis of patch systems but they may offer the kind of structure which Parsloe advocates. They encourage flexibility and professional discretion, yet within the local authority constraints. More importantly they offer, by their emphasis on *local* interdisciplinary teamwork the opportunity for social workers to share problems and hence anxieties with the people who are also involved in child abuse. Specialist child care teams, on the other hand, cover a larger geographical area leading to more isolation and a more restricted set of relationships; this is especially true in the investigation phase of child abuse work when anxieties are at their highest.

No structure can create complete relief from anxiety. However a structure which is too rigid or remote, too much of a Role Culture, may deprive the social worker of the support and reassurance that familiar local colleagues can provide. Hence the wise SSD will recognise that stress in child abuse work comes not only from the clients but also from the agency work setting.

Feelings

When the more extreme cases of child abuse attract media attention it is individual social workers who are criticised more than SSDs. It is not surprising then that individual emotions run high. Social workers are more than mere officials; they bring into child abuse a range of feelings which need consideration.

It may seem too obvious to state that worker feelings may be almost exclusively negative in this area and that very little of the actual work is straightforward or pleasant; however, an impression is that qualifying and then in-service training has tended to skirt such issues and rely on standard levels and methods of supervision and support backed by codes of practice. Most of the time, child abuse is something that social workers would prefer not to do and it is perhaps surprising and gratifying that there have not been more mistakes.

'Getting it right' will depend ultimately on the worker possessing a personal psychic framework which can sustain planned work in the face of external hostility and inner tension. Such issues, which underly good practice, will make sense to the more experienced social worker but all frontline staff will, we hope, seek ways and the framework to raise their anxieties with their peers and their managers. SSDs will vary in the extent to which they make this possible. The more mechanistic and 'role-culture' influenced the organisation, the less it will be able to allow for individual needs.

The child abuse incident is not only a crisis for the child and family but also for the agency and its staff who deal with it. In the short term the right kind of response may not require the allocation of extra finance or the relocation of material resources; rather we can talk about raised awareness, the resurrection of some 'dying' theories and the development of real staff-supervision skills in first-line managers.

Role conflicts

Although there is considerable literature about roles, how well do social workers understand the conflicts they face in child abuse? In other areas of work there is often a choice, or at least, a range of roles, often rewarding. For example: advocacy is often something which is well understood by both client and worker; once agreed it is possible for the worker to implement it with reasonable clarity in dealing with other agencies. In child abuse on the other hand, the range of roles often interplay awkwardly and are not always seen as clear or distinctive by clients, other agencies and even the workers themselves. Thus there is potential for confusion both internally and externally. Payne (1982, p. 52) has listed a string of roles which various authors have suggested for social work and those in child abuse inevitably cluster at the 'hard' end.

Agency procedures rarely acknowledge possible role conflict, leaving individuals to find their own coping mechanisms to handle the inner stress. How do they do this? Firstly, they may react to multiple roles by playing down or even ignoring one and pursuing others exclusively, even obsessively. For example, the advocate role can be an attractive one which relegates those of inspector or therapist. At other times, a worker may convince himself that a family really will respond to treatment, make them over-dependent on him and fail to look for signs of ill-treatment. In one example known to us, an allegation of ill-treatment was dealt with by a very intelligent social worker who had a reputation for doing very intensive family therapy work with many of his clients. His initial visit lasted over two-and-a-half hours and his subsequent report was a mass of detail about the family's complex dynamics. Unfortunately, he failed even to confront the parents with the allegation and another worker had to be sent back to the family to do this! Conversely there may be social workers who may be over-zealous inspectors because they lack other skills, or worse, have unrecognised authoritarian tendencies.

The social worker's problem comes from the fact that he is not a free agent able to select certain roles rather than others; he is ultimately a member of an organisation which is faced with the legal dilemmas of care, protection and control. It can, therefore, happen that workers may resort to coping mechanisms that are unhealthy – denial, displacement, dilution of all roles, cynicism and even alcohol. The employing agency needs to be aware of this and, as we discuss below, has to provide sensitive support for its front line staff.

Role problems are compounded by the expectations of other agencies and clients themselves. Few people may actually be aware of what social workers do, what they can do and what they cannot. The huge increase in Place of Safety Orders in the mid-1970s may say much about the expectations of forces outside social work itself and may suggest that social workers are 'social policemen'; it may in the process obscure other equally important roles. While the regular use of inter-disciplinary case conferences has increased mutual understanding, it may not always highlight the individual differences in social workers which may be masked by a 'role-culture' policy.

Power and authority

The attention focused on child abuse can encourage myths about the power of social workers, for example that the placing of a child's name on the At Risk Register gives the *right* of visiting and entry to the family's home. The family themselves may accept and operate under this illusion and social workers may utilise this ignorance if they feel the ends are justified. Other agencies will often forget that the removal of children invokes a legal role which is (or should be) dependent on evidence which a court would find reasonable.

Again it is not always clear to an alarmed paediatrician that social workers will normally struggle to combine the role of care (by arranging substitute care for a child) with rehabilitation or at least linking the child with the natural family. Another myth is that case conferences make 'decisions' which then provide a legal clarity and sanction for subsequent social worker activities.

Faced with such pressures social workers may over-visit a family, (play-safe), under-visit (avoidance) or succumb to whatever is the greatest area of pressure. They may themselves lose sight of the roles they are occupying and alternate haphazardly. This may be at great cost and in professional and personal isolation. To outsiders this may confirm the old opinion that social workers lack specific skills and it requires more than clear agency procedures to dispel this.

Personal values and attitudes

How do social workers feel when confronted with child abuse? We have already suggested that there are important subjective elements which are important in day-to-day work especially where families are already known. Dale (1983) talks of the problem of 'enmeshment' and of the 'dangerous social worker' whose involvement with a family may make objective assessments difficult. Moore (1983) has referred to research about the relationship between victims, aggressors and investigators where complex, often unconscious, processes are at work.

Multiple roles and worker values can produce various permutations. At a conscious level this may work through empathy and at the unconscious level through identification, or the lack of it, with clients. For example, a worker may well be able to empathise with a family who ill-treat their child physically on impulse and may feel some sympathy. Faced with pre-meditated sexual abuse over a long period he may feel very differently. We know of one case where a mother who was an ex-nurse adminstered small amounts of poison to her baby daughter over a period of months before she was detected. This form of abuse clearly required calculated, cool planning, the ability to tell lies convincingly and to exploit the fact that the mother and the helping agencies shared similar educational and social positions.

A crucial factor will often be the level of the worker's self-knowledge. An action we cannot contemplate doing may stimulate fear, anger, disgust and even curiosity. An action nearer to our own experience may lead to entirely different feelings – sympathy, sadness or perhaps over time even a sense of comradeship. A social worker who has lived with a family's struggles for months might find himself saying, 'Look, I know it's awful, but my bosses have asked me to check up on this. . . .' Social workers must find the honesty to admit that they need someone outside themselves who is aware of such mechanisms. Without support they remain on a dangerous dimension where at one end they may be unnecessarily cold or hostile towards clients or, at the other end, they may over-identify and be lulled into a false sense of security. Ironically, the high levels of anxiety that exist about child abuse can aggravate these problems, especially where workers feel impelled to visit families too frequently and become caught up in over-ambitious therapies; they can then have too big a vested interest in the treatment method succeeding. Any slippage by the family may then be denied because it represents task failure.

The need for support

We have argued that social workers find child abuse very painful because it is a subjective business, carried out under a mantle of very stressful role conflicts, and the conflicting expectations of clients, other agencies and the public. To cope with this they need to establish and monitor a core foundation of attitudes towards child abuse which reflect practice experience and shape it and which can also withstand examination by others. Secondly, and linked to personal attributes, workers need to be objective about their feelings, and have an idea about their source and how the feelings affect other people.

Appropriate supervision and support is always a two-way process but in this chapter we are mainly concerned about the needs of the frontline workers. Previous sections have suggested four main areas in which social workers are likely to need help:

1. Coping with their personal attitudes, values and anxieties.
2. Coping with role conflicts both within themselves, within their agencies and with other agencies.
3. Making assessments about possible child abuse that are realistic, appropriate and reasonable.
4. Making decisions which represent a balance between personal professional responsibility and agency rules and procedures.

Qualities of supervisors

The first quality we would seek is *openness*. Social workers need to feel confident that they can approach their supervisor to explore issues and admit negative feelings. Child abuse work can produce very strong anxieties and personal doubts which must be acknowledged and worked with. Some social workers cope better than others and there may be a feeling, through professional pride, that people should soldier on even when they are floundering. A distant supervisor who has a formal supportive role which is not properly accepted or implemented makes himself inaccessible to his staff. Most SSDs lay much emphasis, formally, on the almost exclusive line between practitioner and team leader in terms of case discussion; while peer-group consultation is an important and common feature in good teams, the particular anxieties of child abuse work force the practitioner to be very dependent on good support from above. Openness and accessibility require both the right kind of attitude as well as a proper structure for consultation through regular sessions between worker and supervisor.

Openness in supervisors is clearly an aspect of concerned, caring management. Caring is a quality we expect to find in social workers and the supervisor perhaps needs to offer the same standards to one of his team members that he would expect that person to demonstrate towards clients. Thus, the social worker's negative feelings should be accepted without rejection and handed back as energy for renewed motivation. It may seem superfluous to restate such basic values but we are aware that many team leaders in present SSDs can be attracted and encouraged towards a more 'managerial' style where the major concerns are staff organisation and deployment, resource allocation, agency representation and the development of team policies and strategies. These are important tasks in a large welfare agency as long as they do not take place at the expense of the more traditional roles of team leaders, individual staff supervision and consultation; these may remain, unexamined, in the job description and occupy a low priority. If this is the case the organisation needs to consider whether such roles should be formally re-allocated to other staff, senior practitioners for example. What is important is that the social worker has proper access to help.

A second quality desirable in supervisors is *counselling ability*. As a reaction against the darker side of a psycho-analytic approach towards frontline staff by supervisors – 'Tell me, what do your angry feelings *really* say about yourself?' – there has been a tendency for staff to insist they are not treated like clients. This smacks of arrogance; the social worker who cannot sleep at night because he thinks he has stumbled upon a child abuse case may have *exactly* the same difficulties and needs as many of his clients. There is no shortage of counselling literature (see Gilmore, 1973; Egan, 1980; Nelson-Jones, 1982–3) or even courses, and supervisors can also find ways to reinforce their interview skills (see Maple, 1977). A possible value of counselling techniques is that historically they have been used in a very wide range of situations with a large cross-section of help-seekers so that they are more free of some of the undertones attached to casework.

Allied with counselling and interview skills the supervisor needs knowledge of *psychology* (particularly regarding stress and motivation), *staff management* and *assessment skills*. A management approach which encourages the delegation of more responsibility to subordinates is valuable because it is likely to help clients and demonstrate to other agencies that they are dealing with those who are professionally and personally mature and confident. Attempts by managers and supervisors to hold on to as much responsibility as possible produce powerless workers who lack credibility for other agencies or clients. The recent research of client perceptions of their workers by Sainsbury *et al.* indicates that agency position and individual worker skills have a fluid relationship to each other. Hence:

> Thus, extensively among clients and to a less extent among workers, some kind of dissociation was assumed to exist between worker and agency, reminiscent – in practical terms – of broader disputes about reconciling the roles of professional and employee (Sainsbury *et al.*, 1982, p. 175).

So the psychology of trust and delegation is an important element in helping the supervisor to understand how much rein to give to practitioners. This depends on the ability to *assess*, at second hand, case matters, but, at first hand, the quality of the practitioner's evidence and reports about a case. It is not always necessary for a supervisor to be a specialist to recognise that a worker's own assessment is logical or soundly based.

Because SSDs have so many functions, role confusion exists as a potential problem and, as we have suggested, this may be aggravated by strong anxieties in child abuse. Thus, the supervisor needs some appreciation of *role theory and models*. Payne's very practical book *Working in Teams* (Payne, 1982, esp. chs 4, 5 & 6) provides a manual which ought to reside permanently on team leaders' desks. Not only does it explore agency and worker roles, it also discusses methods of identifying and developing team styles and strategies. Knowledge of roles is an essential tool for staff supervision particularly where, as we have seen, practitioners may select, not always consciously, some roles rather than others. A wise supervisor will also consider whether the various roles demanded by a child abuse situation could not better be shared amongst several workers, for it is often the pressure to perform well, in a number of functions and at differing levels of complexity, which can exhaust individuals.

General practitioners are not expected to cope alone with their sick patients; just as they work with consultants, hospital nurses, district nurses, physiotherapists, so social workers can be helped to see that what Briggs has termed 'episodes of service' (Briggs, 1980, pp. 36–8) require differing roles and skills rather than 'one case, one worker'. Just because child abuse cases are, rightly, seen as 'difficult' it does not mean that all the work with them involves intensive social worker activity. A family aide, a playgroup leader, a neighbour or a social work assistant may all have important potential roles.

Team leaders as first-line managers are important in organisational terms, being the gateway between practice and policy. Thus they have a significant role as *buffers and communicators*. In a sense they may be at the boundary between role and task cultures for they need to maintain their staff's work in relation to agency policy and procedures but they are also uniquely responsible for encouraging the kind of individual responsibility and creativity that one looks for in practitioners. In child abuse terms this bridging task is very difficult. Most SSD guidelines fail to spell out precisely where the practitioner's duties begin and end – they could hardly do otherwise. Supervisors, therefore, need a keen awareness of organisational dynamics, the law and the possible variations within these for individual practice. At times they need to protect workers from their own agency! A feature of child abuse alarms is the tendency of whole SSDs to shudder, to over-react and to 'zoom down' to the practice level. We have experience of a child abuse referral which involved, in one day, seven different SSD staff at five different hierarchical levels. Only one of them – the social worker – was actually visiting the family! The buffer role is thus a valuable support, particularly where there are outside pressures too.

Directions for supervision

The previous section contains somewhat scattered references to issues for staff who directly supervise social workers in SSDs. Do they provide a basis for some kind of framework for supervision?

While the media and perhaps the public find it more convenient to blame individual workers when children are abused there are signs at the time of writing of a greater acknowledgement by official circulars and inquiries that poor supervision is as vital in child abuse work as practitioner activity: the Beckford report (1985, ch. 21) devotes a chapter to supervision, BASW contemporary Guidelines (BASW, 1985) gives as much space to managers and supervisors as to practitioners, the DHSS Review of Child Care Decisions (DHSS, 1985c) summarises research concerns about policy and supervision problems and the Social Services Inspectorate (DHSS, 1986b) report of nine SSDs is concerned exclusively with supervision.

Drawing freely from the above it is possible to identify a number of tasks for supervisors in their work with practitioners. These arise from three key roles: representing and interpreting agency policy, monitoring work and providing advice and personal support.

Supervision tasks

● To know and communicate agency policy and procedures in child abuse.
● To know and communicate the levels at which decisions are made in the agency.
● To distinguish between the general managerial role and the supervisory role.
● To distinguish between supervision and consultation.
● To offer a planned individual programme of supervision.
● To distinguish between 'reactive and scheduled supervision' (DHSS, 1986b, p. 30).
● To monitor work through reading of case files and the review of decision implementation.
● To record decisions and recommendations, made through supervision, in case files.
● To offer advice and information about legal and professional matters.
● To arrange specialist consultation and support from elsewhere (where the supervisor undertakes this himself he should acquaint himself with relevant literature on child abuse (Beckford Report, 1985, esp. pp. 205–7, 218, 293).
● To ensure that child abuse work is allocated only to practitioners who are suitably qualified and experienced

(where this does not happen it should be recorded in the case files).

● To monitor and control practitoners' workloads to minimise stress.
● To explore and monitor practitioners' personal feelings regarding child abuse cases.
● To anticipate the stress caused by child abuse work and to offer appropriate personal and professional support.

It is a feature of organisations that frontline tasks are more often defined in detail than the work of others. A properly codified set of procedures and guidelines would serve two purposes: to identify accountability better and to provide much needed reassurance for practitioners.

Staff development

The best form of staff development is staff protection. By this we mean that practitioners, particularly when they are new and inexperienced, are less likely to develop if they are exposed too quickly and haphazardly to too much work. We regret a 'tribal initiation' model where the poor manager tests staff by throwing them in at the deep end to see if they sink or swim. The first child abuse referral, just like the first Mental Health Act 'section', may be treated as an initiation test. The novice is stripped of protection and sent out into the desert of child abuse to see if he survives. The point about such primitive tribal initiation rituals is that they involve a test of personal strength and suffering often experienced in total isolation in the wilderness. This will probably ring familiar bells for many social workers.

When this happens, it may be that supervisors are merely repeating practices that they themselves experienced in their early careers; or distance from the front line may blunt supervisors' awareness of the particular stresses of child abuse work and they may come to believe that all the social worker has to do is follow procedures. Again, child abuse work accounts, numerically, for a very small part of SSD activity (a *Community Care* survey suggested less than one per cent of new cases in 1982 'for the majority of its respondents (*Community Care*, May 1983, p. 19) and it is understandable if team leaders are often distracted by other pressures on their time.

For the reasons above, and there will be others, we may have a situation where there is a lack of care for the carers.

In-service training

Why is it that child abuse has commanded a great deal of concern and yet resulted in very patchy tangible support for staff within SSDs? Why have approved Social Workers been introduced in mental health work but not in child abuse? Why should preparation for mental health work require formal in-service training leading to nationally organised examinations and yet child abuse training be left to the whims of SSDs? Whatever the reasons – and we are inclined to believe they are political – some social workers must see the situation as paradoxical where high expectations of frontline staff are combined with a lack of agency will, commitment or resources to offer support.

However, we know of examples of positive policies and very practical support for staff. For example, Brown has described in detail how two Merseyside SSDs combined to develop training courses aimed at improving knowledge and skills about the social work roles of therapist, inter-agency worker, investigator and case conference chairing. Often these courses have been offered to staff of various agencies using joint-funded money and utilising the treatment skills of local NSPCC staff. In one case the money was provided to enable a staff member to undertake the Open University Course on abuse in families. Brown summaries his report by saying:

> The organisation of such an intensive training programme devoted to just one area of the work of a busy department demanded a considerable commitment in time. There is evidence that the investment is reaping dividends, demon-strated by improved co-operation between workers from different agencies, greater self-confidence of staff and by improved standards of professional practise (Brown, 1983, p. 35).

In a personal communication Brown (1984) also pointed to the value of the British Association for the study and prevention of Child Abuse and Neglect (BASPCAN) of which he is a member.

Cleveland SSD provided an example of similar approaches to the problem of developing worker knowledge. In conjunction with Newcastle Polytechnic's Social Work Department, a five-day course was run very much based on Open University course material; this lays heavy emphasis on role-plays, games and simulations and it has been said that the course has increased 'individual workers' confidence, interest and ability to assess levels of risk' (Richardson, 1984). In addition we were told of a two-day course which uses the work of the Rochdale NSPCC Special Unit as its model. 'This course took a systemic view of child abuse within the family, agency and inter-agency systems. Therapeutic principles developed at the Rochdale Unit were presented as a model of assessment and treatment. The emphasis was that procedures and knowledge of risk factors, although fundamental, are in themselves not enough to avoid dangerousness and produce change' (Richardson, 1984).

The correspondent acknowledged that the Rochdale model is controversial, but the important point is that social workers were apparently offered a distinctive, action-orientated approach which could be brought back and tested in their work. Similarly there are important developments in what we might call 'community social work' (to use the Barclay Report term) which could provide useful sources for in-service training. The detailed account of the work of the Harlesden community team (1979), the unitary model, patch team development described by Currie and Parrot (1981) and the rich vein of literature about Holman's voluntary work on a Bath council estate (Holman, 1981) all contain concepts and practical suggestions for social workers to build on. It is important that staff development concentrates on the task culture as well as the role culture. Child abuse official guidelines sometimes have the same dire style as civil defence leaflets on the nuclear holocaust and can heighten anxiety. Social workers need to have encouragement and feedback about positive approaches that may actually improve their practice as helpers. Some agencies are tackling this problem but others clearly are not and the occasional annual conference or seminar is not enough. At another level, social work teams need to find or be encouraged to find, space for child abuse training as part of staff development sessions. The more intimate setting of a team may enable a frank release and exchange of social workers' feelings and we know of teams who adopt specific models of practice and where work sharing is encouraged.

Assessment

If staff can develop under a proper mantle of positive protection they also need some form of open, structured feedback about their work. The label 'Approved Social Worker' is now seen, for all its teething troubles, as a recognition of individual skills. We are not happy about the rather primitive reliance on the written examination, but would welcome the principle in other areas of work including child abuse (preferably as part of a wider theme of 'work with children and their families'). Post-qualification or in-service courses provide an opportunity for assessment.

In addition we would support routine, standardised assessment schemes for staff; these should be concerned with *general* developments in a worker's activities conducted in a similar way to reviews of cases. We would expect them to be done by the team leader, although there is no reason why some other designated staff member should not do this; there might be merit in the idea of such a person developing expertise in this area. It is important that any staff assessment is able to account for fluctuations in worker ability. A criticism of I.Q. tests is that the final overall score conceals a range of abilities. Therefore, a social worker assessment could perhaps be based on a list of roles and their respective methods and skills as well as more general activities. Thus, a social worker who had had a child abuse case go wrong might be found to be weak on inter-agency liaison; he might, at the same time, be a very competent investigator or skilled in generating resources to support families. A sensitive assess-

ment document will make useful statements about perform-
ance rather than personalities.

Assessment can also be used as a method of team
communication and development. Currie and Parrott describe a system of nine monthly assessments to which various
team members can contribute and Brill (1976) in her work of
teams suggests structures for exploring individuals' contributions and roles within teams. The increasing interest in team
dynamics and shared responsiblity contrasts with the rather
isolated case-bound experiences of many teams researched
by Parsloe *et al.* (1978). Good assessments can achieve
several results:

● identify weak and strong areas
● suggest ways to increase knowledge and skills
● promote real sharing amongst staff
● clarify job descriptions, roles and responsibilities
● re-define relationships between superior and subordinate
● encourage negative feelings to be expressed
● promote work allocation on a logical and explicit basis
● increase a team's awareness of its components.

In effect, an adequate system of staff assessment could
enhance child abuse work by translating generalised anxieties
into specific issues about worker skills and abilities. Where it
is carried out in a team setting it could lead to the kind of
allocation of work which brings the right intervention to the
client at the right time.

Summary

We have concentrated on this chapter on the very sharp end
of social work practice – individual feelings, attitudes and
skills. We have suggested that despite the substantial collective response of SSDs to child abuse, the social worker
frequently finds himself alone and fearful, exposed to severe
stress that may reveal profound aspects of his personality.
Child abuse work highlights with a special intensity the
various role permutations which are a common feature of
most local authority social work. Conflicts can arise both

within and without the worker's own department. Again, the discovery or suspicion of child abuse can arouse strong emotions which may lead to various defence mechanisms in the worker.

It seems clear that workers in such situations need proper support. This is normally the task of team leaders and we urge that they have a clear understanding of their role so that individual staff support as well as wider managerial duties are explicity stated. If this is not possible then support tasks may need to be transferred formally to other staff. What is necessary is an arrangement which allows practitioners to talk about their problems, fears and doubts, openly. We suggest this could profitably be linked to formal staff assessment schemes; the value of this is that it may guard against a tendency for practitioners to feel mass guilt or for their supervisors to indulge in general criticism when things go wrong. Because child abuse work can be so worrying there is a case for dividing up the work more in terms of skills in relation to issues and this is more achievable with a formal assessment scheme.

We have made a strong plea for child abuse work to be given at least the same status as that in the mental health field and wonder why this has not been the case. From here we have argued for more in-service training and given some examples. As we argued earlier in the chapter the task culture aspect of child abuse work remains neglected. Social workers' best defence against fear of child abuse lies in thinking about it beforehand, monitoring existing work and being given the opportunity for reflection afterwards. In the present state of SSD in-service training a little knowledge may be much better than hardly any.

4

Assessing Risk and Taking Risks

If one single word sums up child abuse work it is 'risk'. We talk of children 'at risk' and of social workers 'taking risks' in their decisions about children in their care or under their supervision. Equally, child abuse inquiries have been particularly concerned with re-evaluating definitions of risk and the quality of social work decisions. Much of the literature and research on the subject has tried to discover (without much detailed success) factors, characteristics, situations and patterns which might be used to predict risk to children.

Risks and decisions about them are thus central social work issues. Yet, for all the professional preoccupation, there appears a lack of systematic approaches to the actual mechanics of handling risk; even if risks are identified there still remains, for social workers in particular, a complex process of weighing them against other factors. It is this process which remains at the centre of frontline work and by its nature it can never be fully prescribed by statute or agency guidelines. Without a knowledge of this process there is a danger, as numerous inquiries have found, that decisions about children at risk are more likely to depend on the variable dynamics of inter-disciplinary meetings, value judgements, personal philosophies and even optimism.

Risk analysis

The rest of this chapter will draw heavily on the work of Brearley (1982b) who has made an interesting contribution to the understanding of the risk process. His starting point is that although the notion of risk is complex, it is amenable to analysis and he draws much of his basic material from the field of insurance, where, as one would expect, this concept is of fundamental and practical importance. Brearley has developed and applied his ideas in various contexts (Brearley, 1980, 1982a) and it is therefore possible to consider how child abuse issues can be illuminated by his approach.

Definitions

Several key definitions underpin the concept of risk:

1. *Risk* refers to the relative variation in possible loss outcomes (where loss means an undesriable event).
2. *Probability* refers to the relative likelihood of outcomes.
3. *Uncertainty* refers to the subjective responses of the person who is exposed to risk.
4. *Hazard* refers to an existing factor – an action, event, lack, deficiency or entity – which introduces the possibility or increases the probability of an undesirable outcome.
5. *Danger* refers to a feared outcome of a hazard which is either expected to be a loss outcome or which is associated with loss in the expectation of the observor.
6. *Risk-taking* takes place if the actor is conscious of the risk, if the potential loss is irreversible, and if the exposure to risk is accepted in the hope of a relative gain (or reduced loss) (Brearley, 1982b, pp. 26–7).

These definitions are necessarily detailed. We should also note three things: firstly, that some of the terms are more objective than others. Thus a coin can fall heads or tails, there are no other outcomes, but a gambler will have all sorts of feelings about what *will* turn up. A small irregularity in the table surface might seem a serious hazard to the gambler who is already in debt, whereas a bucket of acid instead of a table is clearly a universal hazard to the coin producing any result at all; secondly, Brearley talks of actors and observors and it should be noted that the social worker can occupy both roles in child abuse – and is, therefore, 'at risk' just as the child is;

the third point to make is that the terms are, as described, linked in a *process* rather than as separate static entities.

Application to child abuse

How do Brearley's ideas work in practice? It is instructive to choose a particular case of a child death where events moved quickly to a tragic conclusion. Gemma Hartwell, a 22-month-old child, was killed by her father in Birmingham in 1985. At the time, remarks made by the chairwoman of the Social Services Committee highlight some of the confused thinking that follows from an *ad hoc* approach to 'risk'. She was quoted as saying that the decision by social workers to return Gemma to her parents while she was still in care was 'wrong', but 'it was a very carefully worked-out decision by caring people who behaved in a reasonable way – although the decision they made turned out to be tragically wrong' (*Social Work Today*, 25 November 1985, p. 10). This actually makes no sense and it is unlikely, for example, that the same comment would be made if an insurance company insured a 22-month-old baby who died of an obscure disease soon after. A better judgement would be that the decision was 'unsuccessful'. Where decisions are carefully based on the best possible estimates they are nevertheless followed by a routine period of 'uncertainty' about the outcomes which could include 'loss' of some kind.

The table opposite is a speculative attempt to consider decisions about Gemma Hartwell in terms of Risk Analysis (though it probably applies to many other cases).

If this is an approximate summary of the situation that faced social workers before they made their decision, it is already clear that we have a mixture of objective facts and subjective impressions. Mr Hartwell *had* previously assaulted children and there was ample evidence of family difficulties. Similarly, the parents' determination to get Gemma back meant that they would be hostile to any plan to place her elsewhere; such a plan would itself expose her to the risk of being in care (which as a feature might itself produce adults who become unsuccessful parents). However, from this point the picture is less clear. Whether or not the social workers

A. *Decision to Return Child to Parents*

Hazards	Dangers
Father's previous offences against children	Stress on Parents
	Stress on Gemma
Family's past difficulties	Stress on Social Workers
Over-optimistic social work assessment	Injury to Gemma

B. *Decision to Keep Child Away from Parents*

Hazards	Dangers
Over-pessimistic social work assessment	Loss of contact with parents
Loss of prospective adopters	Deprivation in Residential Care
Difficulties in placements	Care
Hostility of parents	Rejection of Gemma
Unsuccessful fostering	Stress on Gemma
	Damaged Personality

could correctly evaluate the family is a matter of judgement. As Brearley points out, hazards depend to some extent on assumptions. A nuclear accident is univerally accepted as a hazard but social work hazards are frequently more ambiguous.

The hazards identified so far are all specific to Gemma. The situation is further complicated if we add another level of factors which have been *generally* associated with child abuse – young parents, previous battering incidents, difficult pregnancies, socio-economic category, social isolation. Brearley makes a useful distinction between 'pre-disposing hazards' like these and 'situational hazards' which arise from a particular set of circumstances. Similarly he distinguishes between 'Vulnerable Groups' and 'Endangered Individuals' (Brearley, 1982b, pp. 30–49). It would seem that in the Hartwell case the broader factors were perhaps offset by optimism about specific ones. At the same time, factors which predispose children who come into care to loss (disturbed childhood) were given a lot of weight reinforced by the actual breakdown of Gemma's prospective adoption placement.

Hazards to children

Previously we have challenged the assertions of researchers about particular factors which are said to predispose parents to ill-treat their children. Our view is that there has been a disappointing lack of progress in isolating specific 'causes for the disease'.

In reality social workers may have to content themselves with using much broader predisposing hazards lists about general family difficulties. Thus Gorell Barnes suggests: 'In Great Britain any form of assessment based on a single dimension of family functioning such as communication or affective functioning or behavioural functioning is not in favour.' and she offers the following list:

1. absence of gross distortion of affectional bonds;
2. gross disturbance in the feeling of the family as a secure base from which children can safely explore;
3. absence of gross distortion of parental models which child imitates (consciously or unconsciously) and on which identification is formed;
4. presence of dysfunctional styles of coping with stress (for example, disproportionate aggression; perpetual recourse to illness);
5. absence of interaction or gross distortion in the interaction between parents;
6. absence of necessary and developmentally appropriate life experience (food, warmth, play, conversation and interaction leading to the development of social skills);
7. absent or exaggerated disciplinary techniques;
8. absent or distorted communications network (inside the family and between the family and the outside world) (Gorell Barnes, 1984, pp. 17–18).

These factors are both wide-ranging but also specific enough to explore in individual cases.

A shorter set of family factors is considered by Thorman based on Beaver's work (1977):

Power is either not shared because of conflicts between parents or it is dissipated chaotically.

Autonomy of family members is poorly developed so that boundaries are either too restrictive or too blurred.
Communication is constricted, distorted or confused. Inhibited feelings may prevent family members expressing themselves easily or inadequate skills may simply make understanding difficult.
Negotiation follows from the other factors as a serious problem. Problem-solving depends on secure roles and feelings and clear communication; without these, problems will seem to the family too dangerous or too bewildering to negotiate (Thorman, 1982, ch. 2).

The concept of autonomy is particularly interesting as it echoes a finding reported by various authors (see Cook & Bowles, 1980, esp. pp. 129–316) that abusing parents may see a child at times of stress as a symbol or reflection of their own feelings and needs; they thereby deny or limit that child's autonomy as a growing person.

Thorman sets his family factors within a two-fold model developed by Minuchin who sees disturbed families as either 'enmeshed' or 'disengaged' (Thorman, 1982, pp. 105–7). The first state is characterised by rigidity, power struggles and intensity while the second is more a disintegration into chaos, irresponsibility and neglect.

Identifying broad hazards is obviously essential to any scheme of risk analysis and, in our view, less 'risky' than some of the more controversial indicators which appear in much child abuse literature. Both Gorell Barnes and Thorman implicitly acknowledge the benefits of a general, multiple-cause model. Minuchin's ideas also fit the commonsense view that there are parents who abuse because of intense misperceptions (ill-treatment) and those who do it through a failure to perceive (neglect).

The dynamics of risk

Up to this point the risk analysis offered has concentratred on what could be called 'static' hazards; these are identified through existing knowledge about the past. However, it is clear from further study of the Gemma Hartwell Case that the *situational* hazards increased dramatically once she returned home. The family failed to take her to a daily family centre as they had promised. Although at first they had genuine reasons, this was a hazard because it led to less supervision. A further and consequential hazard was the parents' excuses for avoiding further visits. Here the situation is complex because of the parents' growing fear for discovery and, we assume, the increased tension this aroused in them. We can speculate that this involved them in 'uncertainty' that Gemma might be removed from their care which would certainly have been a 'loss outcome' in their eyes.

Thus, while the original social work decision was to a large extent based on static factors – the family's history and possible disruptions in care – the situation changed dynamically. The case is perhaps exceptional in that Gemma was killed only 16 days after she was returned home but it does illustrate how important it is for events *and their significance* to be monitored closely. Yet intense supervision of families (as we consider later) as was the case for Gemma, may itself create pressure and accelerate a family's slide into crisis.

Although Brearley's basic definition of hazard refers to 'existing factors', a thorough analysis will include *all* influences on the way a family functions. Thus the assumptions, attitudes and activities of all those involved with the family, may increase the risk of a loss outcome. The following extra-family factors are, therefore, important elements in a list of possible hazards:

- deficiencies in support services
- deficiencies in supervision or monitoring
- failures of inter-professional communication
- unclear case-conference decisions
- distraction by other social work cases
- personal stress within the social worker
- political/policy changes within the service agencies
- changes in public opinion
- social work philosophies or ideologies.

Some of these will be predisposing and some will be situational. It is a pity that, in terms of risk analysis, official inquiries have often tended to discuss both kinds of hazards as though they were interchangeable. For this reason, it is difficult to know whether social workers should be criticised because their philosophy is at fault or because they make specific errors of judgement.

Dangers as hazards

It should also be clear from the analysis that what may be a danger (a feared loss outcome) can in turn become a hazard. So a major anxiety for Gemma's social worker was that supervision of the family might be impeded; once this happened it became a hazard to Gemma's well-being – both predisposing in the sense that parents who resist supervision are reckoned to be more dangerous, and situational, in that it was a specific alarm-bell once her parents began to tell lies. This demonstrated how fluid and fast-moving a situation can become particularly where all the participants, whether family or workers, carry anxiety which is easily aggravated.

In order to keep pace with such movement, workers need to maintain good frequent contact with each other so that a situation can be monitored continuously. As we argue previously in considering 'task' and 'role' models of practice, it is the individual frontline decisions of workers that are ultimately more important than the more cumbersome machinery of case-conferences, registers and inter-agency liaison – the suddenness of Gemma Hartwell's death shows this all too clearly.

While it may be difficult to keep pace with a sudden crisis, a more thorough risk analysis might at least help to anticipate difficulties by asking the following questions:

- What are the predisposing hazards?
- What are and might become situational hazards?
- Are the hazards environments, processes or people?
- What are the dangers not only for the child but also for the parents and the workers?
- Can any dangers become in turn, hazards?
- What then are the future dangers from such hazards?

The whole analysis can be done in tabular form and can be

broken down in terms of existing factors, likely factors, events and participants as they affect the process through time. It can be further developed to show *for whom* a loss outcome is feared because the anxieties of participants and their fear loss can threaten further losses to others. Hence a social worker who becomes suspicious because of fresh concerns will have an impact on the behaviour of parents; their increased fear, hostility and guilt may then put the child at greater risk.

Workers as hazards

The Enquiry Report published by Brent (London) Council into the death of Jasmine Beckford is firm and forceful in its belief that the actions and attitudes of various workers and agencies contributed to her abuse. If this is so we can fairly consider them as hazards in terms of risk analysis and produce a table that is said to apply to social workers:

Predisposing hazards

- Over-optimism about the rehabilitation of children with their families
- Over-pessimism about the life of children in substitute care
- Belief in co-operative work with parents
- Over-sensitivity to the needs and feeling of parents
- Reluctance to accept a policing role in child abuse cases
- General difficulties in arranging placements for children
- Variations in Social Services Departments child-abuse procedures
- Lack of shared values with other agencies
- Generic social work training
- Lack of experience

It would be possible to produce similar lists for other workers and agencies who have been criticised by Enquiry Reports – doctors, health visitors, teachers, magistrates who all bring particular viewpoints to child abuse work. Thus the Beckford Enquiry rebuked the Juvenile Court Magistrates for urging the social workers to give priority to Jasmine's return to her parents (Beckford Report, 1985, pp. 98–104). Again it has been reported that GPs as a group have been less willing to attend case-conferences than other workers; this can, therefore, be seen as a predisposing hazard to children being abused.

The point of such a listing is that it enables us not only to survey possible hazards but also to locate them within the network of agencies and individuals who can influence a case. Such an analysis will indicate what action and by whom might reduce hazards. Where Juvenile Courts prove to be particularly sympathetic towards parents who seek their children's return home, a high level approach by social services managers would be appropriate. This kind of detailed analysis of worker/agency predisposing hazards might have brought more benefits than the generally un-orchestrated comments of Inquiry Reports. Where Reports are specific, as in the Beckford Case, action can follow. The Lord Chancellor, for example, has now required that Juvenile Court Magistrates should have more training in child abuse matters related to care proceedings (*Social Work Today*, 28 April, 1986, p. 4).

Where particular cases are concerned, a further list of hazards associated with social workers may prove helpful.

Situational hazards

- Inadequate supervision of family
- Denial of risks to the child
- Failure to detect significant warning signs
- Poor communication with other workers
- Excessive compliance with the views of other workers
- Lack of knowledge about families and children
- Lack of knowledge of the impact of an adverse environment on the families
- Over-optimism about particular families
- Lack of supervision from senior staff
- Confusion about case responsibility or accountability
- Lack of inter-personal skills
- Lack of assessment skills
- Lack of skill in communicating with children
- Lack of local community resource contacts
- *and* Excessive supervision of family.

What is perhaps concerning about this list is the lack of pattern – no one weak area that could easily become a focus of improvement. Skills in direct work with children, for example, are very different from the ability to build up local community contacts with neighbours and other workers, yet both areas of work are important in child abuse cases. Support for social workers was identified as a problem in the Beckford Report (1985, pp. 215–18) and in terms of risk analysis we might, therefore, see the structure of Social Services Departments as a possible hazard! Although the media were happier at the time to report the individual social workers' involvement the Enquiry Report itself ranges far and wide in its criticisms, from the length and content of social work training down to individual failure to respond to clear warning signals. This multi-level focus echoed Guidelines published at the time by BASW (BASW, 1985).

Our list refers to both inadequate and excessive supervision as possible hazards. If we explore this it is evident that each has its own sequence of cause and effect. Although an under-supervised family may slide into a crisis so also can a family perceive the ever-constant presence of workers as a dangerous hazard to their integrity. This can be shown diagrammatically as in Figure 4.1.

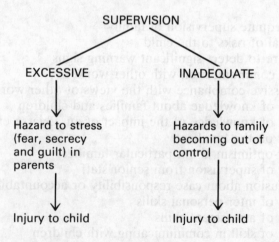

Figure 4.1

Family abuse by workers

Excessive supervision has become a serious hazard in modern social work. A social climate preoccupied with child abuse will produce heightened suspicions in agencies, workers and the general public; this can then become a predisposing hazard to the danger that parents in difficulty may hide their problems out of fear of censure and investigation. There is ample evidence (see Chapter 1) to show that since 1974 compulsory measures to bring into or keep children in care have increased dramatically through Place of Safety Orders, Care Orders, Parental Rights Resolutions and Wardship applications. We run a serious risk that concern has become counter-productive. Extreme examples may even produce the kind of protest which led to the formation of a group called Parents Against Injustice (PAIN) who were victims of wrong allegations of abuse (see *Community Care*, 6 February, 1986, pp. 20–2, and BBC2 'Open Space' documentary, 17 March, 1986).

The dilemma of supervision – not too little, not too much – indicates that workers walk a moral and practical tight rope. Risk analysis based on a systematic exploration of hazard – danger associations points, in some cases, to families being harassed into serious stress in exactly the same way that suspicious over-bearing parents can drive their children into withdrawal and secrecy.

The following case examples illustrate the 'steamroller' of child abuse investigation procedures as they gather momentum and subject families to intolerable pressure.

Case A

A teenage mother presents her very young son at hospital casualty with severe facial burns. The immediate medical prognosis is worrying. The child nearly suffered severe eye damage. The wounds may need skin grafts. The mother's explanation is slow and halting. 'The child fell off a chair onto a gas fire.' She does not inspire confidence in any of the hospital staff who talk to her or who observe her with her child.

Mother and child are admitted to hospital, on a ward where there are many children with similar injuries, with their parents. Mother has already created suspicion. Her speech, behaviour and apparent indifference and occasional anger mark her out for increased observation. The mother, a young working-class girl who has been in Care herself, has the unfortunate luck to be on a ward where most of the other parents seem to be 'concerned, articulate and middle-class'.

Within a few days, a meeting is called to consider placing the child's name on the child abuse register. Only one person present has seen the child and mother at home recently. She is the health visitor, who has a number of positive things to say. The other people present either know the woman from some time ago, her own period in Care, or they have only seen her in hospital. Pictures of the injuries are passed around. They cause revulsion and fear. The fact that the child has made a rapid recovery and that the medical prognosis is now excellent is not given any prominence. The mother's stilted, reluctant explanation of the injury, and her behaviour on the ward lead to an early decision to place the child's name on the register, although the only real 'investigation period' has centred on the post-admission events, and the lack of previous knowledge is not highlighted, despite the health visitor's comments.

Later, the social worker finds out that the mother is living in absolute poverty, and that she was not even present when the accident had occurred. A babysitter had ignored the child's behaviour and had not been able to prevent a fall.

The mother refuses to be involved at all with social services. She will only accept limited advice from the health visitor. At the next meeting, this refusal to co-operate is the main concern. The health visitor continues to make positive statements about the care of the baby and its relationship with its mother. Mother's embarrassment at her poverty and her reluctance to blame her friendly babysitter, and the way these factors influenced her stilted, inarticulate explanation at the outset are apparently put to one side.

Because no one was brave enough at the outset to hold the reins of anxiety and ask for more time to investigate, the mother now finds herself in a 'no win' position. If she cooperates with social services, the obvious implication is that there was 'something wrong' at the outset. If she continues to refuse to co-operate, as is her right, then the only real information that the 'monitoring group' has tends to reinforce their anxieties and not dispel them. The social worker cannot win either. He knows that the child would remain on the register forever, and that there may never be an opportunity for the majority of the participants in the child abuse machinery to make positive statements.

If the child is injured again, or if it injures itself, will the mother feel able to seek appropriate help? No one feels confident about this, but no one is prepared to dismantle the steamroller which has driven us all remorselessly to this point.

Here, the hazard–danger sequence is very clear, particularly in the mother's understandable refusal to accept supervision which she saw as excessive. Further, the importance attached to the mother's unsuccessful explanation of the injuries demonstrates one of Brearley's basic points that hazard definition often depends on value judgements.

Case B

A school teacher makes a report to a school doctor that a boy of 13 appears to be acting strangely. He is often sleepy, looks unwell and not 'with it' much of the time. The boy's parents are not consulted. Instead, the information is passed through to a child abuse unit and an urgent meeting of all those who have some knowledge of the family is called.

At this meeting it is revealed that both parents are known drug users. One is an addict, the other a user. The boy's behaviour is attributed to the use of drugs. It is felt that neither parent would discourage this, assuming that they knew about it.

The boy's name is placed on the child abuse register. No one, except the social worker, seriously questions whether or not this is child abuse, even assuming that the diagnosis of behaviour is correct and that the parents know about it. Does this mean that any child who uses or abuses drugs, with or without parental knowledge, should fall foul of this machinery?

Further meetings reinforce the information base. The police take a strong lead in supplying 'relevant' information. No one is any clearer about what is transpiring between parents and child, but this doesn't seem to matter.

From the outside of the goldfish bowl, the only relevant fact seems to be that all this activity is taking place at a time when the national and local spotlight is firmly fixed on hard drug abuse. Even if we assume that the parents have full knowledge of the child's supposed activities, is this really child abuse? Are parents who allow their children to smoke under age guilty of child abuse? Are residential staff who allow such practices also guilty of similar acts?

The simple answer is that 'it all depends . . .'! Once again the child abuse machinery has become the depository of adult anxiety.

This case illustrates broad as well as practice dilemmas for the social worker. Excessive public anxiety becomes a hazard to the danger of practitioner panic.

Where the definition of child abuse becomes too wide, the perspective for decision-making blurs; anxiety which is likely to follow is clearly a hazard if it inhibits calm, clear thinking and upsets the balance between persecution and negligence.

Strengths in risk-taking

Our analysis thus far has concentrated on hazards. Child abuse inquiries have, unfortunately, followed the same path, perhaps because it is always easier after a tragedy to identify what went wrong rather than what might have gone right. Both the Colwell and Beckford Enquiries (which received extraordinary publicity) concluded that where social workers saw good reasons (strengths) for returning the children to their parents, then arguments were based more on an over-optimistic philosophy than on sound evidence.

If this was true in 1974 it seems hard to believe that eleven years later and almost thirty Enquiries later on, the same applies (general evidence about tougher social work attitudes towards families was completely ignored by the Beckford

Enquiry [see especially pp. 216 and 217]). But it is unfair and unhelpful to blame the Enquiries entirely.

The central question is why social workers have not apparently been able to convince others that they have good evidence (in their own judgement) for preferring child rehabilitation to separation. It might be that the positive factors in a situation need to be systematically catalogued as strengths in terms of risk analysis. Making arguments more coherent and explicit is both good practice and better protection for social workers in the event of outside scrutiny.

The following example shows how to underpin a decision to allow a new baby to remain at home.

Hazards	Strengths
(pre-disposing/situational)	Introduction to parenting
Young parents	skills group
Difficult pregnancy	Early or frequent after-
Reluctance towards	care by health services
supervision	Use of volunteer worker
Social isolation	Sensitive help or
Poverty	supervision by social
Marital Difficulties	worker
Mother in care as a child	Well-trained and
Many workers concerned	experienced social
Sudden deterioration in	worker
the family situation	Development of informal
Etc.	social networks
	Name on at risk register
	Regular case conferences
	Clear worker/agency
	responsibilities
	Good communication at
	practitioner level
	Etc.

Once hazards are identified, whether existing or anticipated, counter-measures can be catalogued and they thus become strengths. The value of this approach is that it encourages detailed as well as creative planning to allocate specific resources and tasks to particular problems as they emerge. If the analysis is set out in enough detail it can become a large-scale working map to include facts, opinions and the perceptions of participants; this will of course include the family and their likely reaction to the logistics of supervision. In tabular form such an analysis could be circulated and would make more sense than the narrative prose which currently emerges from most case conferences. The document could also indicate clearly those areas where 'uncertainty' remains despite best efforts.

The problem of accessible systematic information and assessment is still an issue in child abuse. The 1986 DHSS guidelines contain a report from its Inspectorate (DHSS, 1986b, ch. III & Recommendations) based on a survey on nine SSDs which identified this and the DHSS Review of child care research also saw a need for better methods of recording family histories (DHSS, 1985c, pp. 13–14 and 21).

Summary

This chapter has introduced and explored the concept of risk analysis and found it to be useful in child abuse situations. The notion of a *dynamic* hazard-danger sequence has linked predisposing and situational factors not only within and around families, but also on the worker networks which impinge on them. Both inadequate as well as excessive intervention can create dangers of additional stress on families and we have tried to show the different paths these take.

Risk analysis offers an opportunity to produce explicit detailed plans for action. Written documents can be constructed from Case Conferences and circulated to all participants. When strengths are set against hazards it becomes easier to justify decisions and subsequently to monitor the consequences. In this way social workers may be better able to cope with remaining areas of uncertainty and thus carry on the essential business of taking risks.

As Brearley shows, there are four basic questions to ask when faced with uncertainty.

What are the various possibilities?
How probable are they?
How grave are they?
How imminent are they? (Brearley, 1982b, p. 58)

The answer to each question encompasses attitudes, values, fact, knowledge, calculation and a sense of timing – a complex mix that makes prediction impossible without rigorous analysis and, of course, a degree of good luck.

5

Social Workers as Investigators

The legal position

Child abuse investigation has come to involve numerous agencies and workers. Yet, uniquely amongst them, only the SSD has a *legal duty* towards children in this field. Such a duty is, in fact, shared with the police but the SSD is not constrained by the question of whether a crime may have been committed.

It is this distinctive feature of their local authority context which has a greater influence on social workers than anything else; more than their treatment philosophies, theories of intervention or personal style. The local authority social worker cannot take action based simply on a professional assessment; the action has to be rooted in law which, in practice, means in accordance with legal definitions which are testable in court.

The duty to investigate allegations that children are being ill-treated is set out in Section Two (subsection one) of the Children and Young Persons Act 1969. Somewhat tortuously, the criteria for investigating are those defined in the first section of this act and which are grounds for bringing a child before a juvenile court in his own interests. There are two key elements in this duty to investigate: firstly, the SSD must make enquiries unless these appear unnecessary, and secondly, it cannot pass on the overall responsibility to anyone else. Thus, if telephone enquiries reveal that the child who is subject of the investigation is perfectly safe and well the SSD can decide to take no further action. However, should it decide otherwise and ask a health visitor, for example, to visit the child and his family, it must ensure that it receives a report about the visit; the health visitor is no more than the SSD's agent in this respect and cannot assume or be asked to accept legal responsibility.

Investigation may open the door to other SSD powers and responsibilities – support for the child and family at home, reception into voluntary care, removal on a place of safety order, a wardship application or the initiation of care proceedings to bring the child before the juvenile court in his own interests. All of these are formal processes designed to offer protection to children but only within legally defined limits, and other agencies do not always understand how important these definitions are.

The NSPCC is involved in child abuse investigations but this is a power rather than a duty, a crucial difference. The police also do important work in family crises but their priority is to prosecute offenders rather than to care for victims. However, in the matter of subsequently bringing children before the juvenile court the situation is more complex and an excellent summary is available in the 1985 DHSS Review of Child Care Law (DHSS, 1985a). The NSPCC and the police have the power to bring proceedings subject to certain conditions and the local education authority has a duty where a child has not been attending school. The SSD has a general duty to bring care proceedings but this is not absolute even where the evidence of abuse is strong if the SSD believes that proceedings are neither in the child's nor in the public's interest (Section 2(2) CYP Act 1969). Although in practice it is the SSD which initiates the great majority of care proceedings the possible involvement of other agencies is confusing; this has been recognised (DHSS, 1985a, p. 82 and para. 12.16) and it may be that the law will be modified in the future.

What is undeniable is that where a local authority social worker receives a complaint about a child's welfare his only safe course is to accept full responsibility within his agency's procedures for ensuring that a proper enquiry continues until he is satisfied that the child's welfare has been safeguarded.

Who is the client?

In terms of child abuse investigation it is quite clear, legally, that the client is the child. The law says nothing whatsoever about parents or caretakers per se being the responsibility of local authority social workers (the position in Scotland is significantly different because Section 12 of the Social Work Scotland Act 1968 lays a duty on Social Work Departments to promote the welfare of individuals, not just children). Thus an investigation must confine itself to the condition of the child while the parents should only be seen as a factor in the risk analysis. The law is not concerned that the family is at risk, only the child.

Such apparent clarity should reassure the authors of the Beckford Report for although their concern was with children already in compulsory care, the investigation issue is still relevant. They asserted, 'social workers are not trained (as they should be) to recognise clearly that in their work with children in care, it is the children and not the parents who are their primary concern' and again, 'if and when a choice must be made between the parents' *wishes* and the child's *interests*, the choice must be in favour of the child, even if it is against the parents' (our italics) (Beckford Report, pp. 293–4). This is right, but like the law it cannot be treated in isolation. Just as there are social and cultural contexts for children so also are certain sections of law affected by other sections.

SSDs have many duties and one of them is contained in Section One of the Child Care Act 1980. This aims to prevent children coming into or remaining in care or coming before the Court. By implication, children who are not in care are likely to be living with their parents and where they are young, the various measures of support set out in the section will often involve working through the parents. So it is not that easy, by statute and in practice, for local authority social workers to distinguish neatly between parents and children, between 'wishes' and 'interests'. It is perhaps anomalous that during an era when social workers are constantly urged to seek substitute care more readily, the law continues to assert the importance of preventing care.

The need for balance

Child abuse investigation carries heavy responsibilities. While it may be legitimate for voluntary agencies and workers to adopt partisan views and approaches, SSDs as legal custodians must be careful to avoid their own form of abuse through over-reaction. An allegation may come from a malicious neighbour, an over-anxious school teacher as half-term approaches, an over-zealous paediatrician or local police alarmed by a teenager's spate of delinquency.

The present climate of public anxiety about child abuse has demonstrably generated more referrals to SSDs and Pfohl's (1980) view of abuse as a 'recent discovery' requires social workers to be aware of the wider context of any allegation. The force of the social context is such that the 1986 DHSS Draft Guidelines include, for the first time, a definition of abuse which includes 'potential abuse' (p. 11). In a later chapter they recommend that 'A child's statement that he or she is being abused should be accepted as true until proved otherwise' (p. 25, para 3.3).

These shifts in official policy create fresh problems for the investigating social worker. Potential harm is more difficult to examine than actual harm and any assumption about whether or not children tell 'the truth' may hinder an open and fair exploration of the facts. Maintaining balance and objectivity becomes difficult yet it is essential in everyone's interests.

Balance is also complicated by the fact that SSDs are involved, legally, at every stage in a child's difficulties – from investigation, through court proceedings and on to substitute care. The social worker may therefore have to occupy a number of roles with the risk of overload, ambiguity and conflict. Hilgendorf's (1981) study of social workers in care proceedings provides evidence of this. A pessimistic opinion of the merits of substitute care may discourage a social worker from recognising a dangerous family, or a bitter experience of clashing with magistrates over the disposal of juvenile delinquents may reduce that same worker's readiness to advocate care proceedings. It is no easy matter, it seems, to carry out investigations with the calm detachment that is required.

Social workers as police

If social workers were able to conduct child abuse investigations with little or no concern for the welfare of either the victim or the offender, their task would be much simpler. The police have this advantage in their work. The main criticisms of social workers have been firstly that they lack skill in identifying signs of abuse in children – bruises, impairment in posture or mobility, failure to thrive and behavioural or relationship abnormalities; secondly that their involvement with families may lead them to deny dangers. These are the predisposing hazards earlier discussed.

Would children be better protected if police carried out actual investigations aided, perhaps, by expert medical advice about children's injuries and developmental norms? In some cases the police are involved, especially where they reserve the right to investigate a crime that may lead to prosecution. The NSPCC work closely with the police during their enquiries into sexual abuse and the general policy of inviting police to case conferences allows joint investigations (NSPCC, 1984).

The police are skilled interrogators and this can contribute to child abuse investigations. Medical staff have specialist knowledge about children's health which can be used, yet they have no legal duties in investigations except in the forensic field. It is interesting to speculate why, despite so much criticism of social workers, there have been no proposals to involve other agencies in child abuse investigation. Could it be that no one else wants the job?

For all the difficulties, social workers bring valuable qualities to investigation. Because that investigation is but one part of a process it needs following through within wide considerations. The police have been forced to acknowledge that their enquiries into rape cases have sometimes increased the distress of the victim, whereas social work training encouraged an awareness of the consequences of intervention. It follows that effective therapy does not begin after the investigation but is coincident with it and crisis intervention, which is central to social work training, is very much concerned with processes through time.

Uniquely, SSDs have a comprehensive view of children's needs and the resources they require both at home and elsewhere. Smith has viewed need not so much as an objective entity but as a perception defined by the helping professions (G. Smith, 1980). Although this may prejudice an investigation there is an argument that child abuse as reflecting need should be defined, operationally at least, by an agency which has a tradition of providing protection and care. We can only speculate whether agencies other than SSDs would do a better job of investigation but they would certainly find it difficult to have as wide a perspective.

Effective and efficient investigation

Assessing need

The investigation has two tasks: to identify a condition and then to take the right action to redress it or prevent it. Risk analysis indicates how complex is the first task and the many problems of defining child abuse suggests that the 'condition' is not self-evident. Bradshaw has developed a "taxonomy of need" which employs four categories which are relevant to child abuse:

Normative need: is based on a value standard applied by those in positions of expertise and influence.
Comparative need: is based on the view that if the majority of people (children) enjoy a certain level of basic living, then the minority in similar circumstances who lack those benefits are in need.
Felt need: is discovered by listening to people and asking them what they need.
Expressed need: becomes evident when people take some kind of action to pursue their needs (Bradshaw, 1972).

The Beckford Report provides a good illustration of comparative need when it says 'The simplest test in the world is to put the child on a pair of scales' (Beckford Report, 1985,

p. 70). Data and charts relating to children's development are readily available (see Sheridan, 1975; Fahlberg, 1981; C. Cooper, 1985) and give indications about how society expects its children to grow up and, correspondingly, which children fall below these expectations. The investigating social worker therefore needs some knowledge of developmental norms or access to someone else with the information. Demographic health statistics might suggest that whole regions of children are in need; if so that is a matter for national health policies, whereas the social worker needs to be especially concerned where a child is in need compared to others around him. Assessing felt need and expressed need is more important where emotional abuse is suspected. A teenage girl subjected to sexual harassment by a parent may be afraid to talk about it and the social worker needs considerable counselling skills to enable her to reveal her problem. This will involve creating opportunities for private conversations, perhaps away from home. Younger children may sometimes communicate their fears indirectly and this again demands from the social worker, some familiarity with the way children talk and an ability to create channels for communication both verbal and non-verbal. Sometimes the need may be expressed but through displacement or other defence mechanisms against anxiety and these are clues to possible abuse. The work of Rutter (1975) is rich in discussion of children's psycho-dynamic responses to stress which may form the bulk of evidence in some investigations.

Normative need remains a very difficult practical concept for social workers because it will always reflect society's changing values and moods. Today's norm may be tomorrow's deprivation (shifting views about diet are a good example of this) so that a proactive, predictive approach to child abuse is not truly possible for social work. As the definition of child abuse widens the goal recedes unless we believe that all children are at risk. Abandoning a reactive stance for a proactive one also involves a subtle but important shift in attitudes so that the state rather than the parents is responsible. It may also deter those same parents from seeking help before an investigation is needed.

Views of need must also take account of cultural differences. The more social workers become aware of different cultures and life-styles within society, the more complex is the task of assessing whether a child is in need or at risk. An Asian view of teenage morality may set limits on children which are intolerable to westerners; at what point could this become emotional abuse? We know of a case where a young couple with strong convictions about the dangers of modern convenience food virtually starved their two young children in a firm belief that they were providing a healthy diet. They even challenged conventional developmental weight charts by arguing that they were measures of fat rather than health! Children in care may also face the risk of abuse in cases where SSDs have a policy of placing black children with black foster parents; if they are not available a child may languish in residential care which is only designed for short term work.

Thus need, which underlines investigations and assessment, is not a simple matter. Social workers must improve their knowledge of child development but only within a proper awareness of the wider social context.

Responding to referrals

Heightened sensitivity to child abuse has produced more referrals to SSDs. The initial response can set the tone for subsequent work and should, therefore, be careful and comprehensive. The worker needs to ask who, what, how, where, when and even why of the referrer. People may have ulterior motives for making allegations, beyond a simple concern for truth. We note an abusing family, well-known to an SSD who complained about their next-door neighbours to get their revenge. The night duty social worker, without access to files, made a fruitless and unpopular visit. It is not uncommon for parents in dispute and living apart, to make counter-allegations to further their cases in custody hearings. People with deviant or bizarre life-styles may attract unfair concern from neighbours.

The identity, status or role of an informant may help to assess the value of their information but this certainly does not mean that colleagues and other agencies deserve more attention than others. What behaviour was seen, where and when and how are also important matters to establish when taking a referral. A complaint that a child was hit two weeks ago will mean, if it is true, that any bruises will have faded. Allegations of persistent ill-treatment may mean that a number of molehills, so to speak, are now seen as a mountain. 'She's been treating him badly for ages' needs challenging for further detail. The worker's response needs to be a fine balance between casual acceptance and inhibiting interrogation. Informants may be ambivalent about making complaints of child abuse and easily put off. Even so, the social worker must get as much information as possible. If in doubt he should consider questioning the informant further, especially if the allegation comes by telephone. Following a test case by the NSPCC in 1977, the identity of informants need not be divulged and this can be made clear if they become anxious (House of Lords, 1977).

At times an allegation may hide a complex situation. A parent may threaten abuse out of desperation to get resources or help and other workers may exploit the social workers' fears in order to involve them with a family seen as generally in trouble. Other workers need to be reminded clearly of their moral and professional responsibilities if they make allegations – attendance at case conferences, written reports and even possible appearance in course as witnesses. Such responses may help to filter out misguided or insubstantial allegations.

The importance of time

Child abuse guidelines stress the importance of responding quickly to allegations. How quickly, remains a matter of judgement. In one case two hours may be too long, in another two days may be appropriate. Most families are known to someone and enquiries to other agencies may well produce information which alters the social worker's view of the allegation. If other workers are not available, if a check of files is fruitless and if advice from colleagues is not possible, the next step is unavoidably difficult. To visit or not to visit is a basic social work dilemma that cannot be resolved by written guidelines or the law. It is important, therefore, that the

social worker records carefully the information available, and
steps taken to deal with the allegation initially in order to
justify his action; this is, of course, part of the process of risk
analysis and should show a reasoned sequence of decisions
and actions.

Time used properly can give a worker the opportunity to
think carefully before acting. He may feel that time flies in his
anxiety to respond quickly, but it is unwise to arrive on
doorsteps prematurely. Because child abuse referrals (not
cases) take up a very small part of SSD time, workers may
lack practice; when they do arise a hasty reaction is understandable, however. Time can enable initial impressions to be
re-examined and personal prejudices to be acknowledged.
The support of others at this crucial time is very valuable.

'Dangerous misconceptions'

Just as over-reactions to child abuse are to be avoided, so are
under-reactions. Charles describes common myths held by
workers which may prevent, delay or divert effective investigation:

1. 'Abusing parents will be conspicuously different from
   ordinary parents'; some people, including social workers,
   will have vested interest in thinking the best of parents.
2. 'All must be well if there are no external pressures evident
   on the parents' – this ignores the effects of earlier
   experiences upon current functioning and personality.
3. 'The presence of an apparently unharmed child in a
   household indicates that all children will be safe there' –
   each child has a different personality. Each child therefore
   has the potential to evoke different responses from the
   parents.
4. Abused children are unlikely to be able to offer any critical
   information' – even very young children may find ways of
   communicating their fears and expectations of adults
   (Charles, 1983, pp. 19–21).

Charles discusses another nine similar 'myths' but the list is
extendable by any experienced worker. Misconceptions are
likely to be held by workers who cling too strongly to narrow

views of abuse and who fail to keep up with a wide range of
literature and research.

They also appear in a worker whose over-involvement with
a family blinds him to a deterioration which might seem
obvious to a detached investigator. Over-exposure to incom-
petent and volatile families may also numb a worker's critical
faculties. Alternatively it might be tempting to believe that
other agencies and workers can be relied on to sound the
alarm; their silence may be misinterpreted as 'good news'. If a
family crisis is not properly identified it may be seen as merely
a temporary setback which will get better in time.

There is no sure way to avoid dangerous misconceptions.
Constant vigilance is easier to preach than to practice, and it
may be that the prime responsibility lies not with social work
practitioners but with their supervisors who are detached
enough to ask the right questions and to both support and
monitor their staff.

Information for action

The first part of an investigation is rarely conclusive. This
means that further information is necessary and there are
difficulties about doing this. Should a suspected child be left
alone at home while the worker seeks more information? The
parents' attitude is crucial but may itself depend to some
extent on the way the worker has broached the investigation.
If the child needs to be medically examined and the parents
refuse, the worker has no legal right to carry the child against
their will to a doctor. Since 1977 it has become possible for the
court to make a supervision order with a requirement that the
child be medically examined at the supervisor's discretion
(Rule 28 Magistrates' Courts (Children and Young Persons)
Rules 1970 amended) but this mainly has value, when parents
resist, as evidence in subsequent court proceedings. In the
last resort the worker can only seek a place of safety order to
get immediate control of the child.

In less acute situations it should be remembered that
information may be available from many sources. The official
case conference brings workers together for this purpose but
until it is convened the social worker should explore every

avenue before making any drastic decisions. Formal sources should, where possible, be used alongside informal ones and here the worker with local knowledge may have an advantage in perhaps having contacts who are useful both as informants and as potential sources of help.

Essentially a child abuse investigation concerns itself with parenting. Bentovim suggests three areas to pursue:

the 'level of living' provided for the child
present family functioning
the significance of family history (Bentovim and Bingley, 1985, pp. 45–57),

and we would add 'the significance of the past and present environment'. Such a focus indicates that child abuse is what Kadushin (1981) terms 'an interactional event'. It is more than just an inquiry, a family crisis, a parental collapse in the face of poverty or unemployment, but has to be seen as a dynamic situation that has a past, a present and a future. If anything, it is the future element which is most important for it is possible to argue that if loving parents have a momentary aberration and injure their child, little action need be taken if there is *no* likelihood of it happening again.

To obtain information good enough to make predictions is the most difficult part of child abuse investigations. Such information is unlikely to be available in any certain form but the social worker can at least be systematic, as we have already argued, in setting out, in writing, what is known and what is assumed. In other words an efficient statement and summary of information may be as valuable as the information itself. Investigation depends on very basic skills of data gathering and analysis, and communication with others. In this respect child abuse is no different from any other social work assessment.

Procedural documents lay much emphasis on the proper recording of information about child abuse. Several purposes are served if this is done well. It can become a tool for self-analysis especially where facts are weak and assertions predominate. A supervisor can use records as a check on the worker's earlier verbal information and as a basis for discussion. Case records may later be scrutinised by the SSD lawyer building a court case for which they may be crucial; a guardian-ad-litem appointed by the court in the child's interests as an independent social worker assessor, may study them although he would need the SSD's permission. They may even be demanded for inspection by the court itself. It is worth remembering that some investigations extend over a long period; rather than a single extreme incident, a series of smaller events accumulate concern and precise recording is essential if their significance is not to be missed.

It is becoming common for SSDs to make their case files more accessible to clients and councillors. Apart from the justice of this development it should promote recording which is less speculative and this will benefit child abuse investigation work while still protecting the confidentiality of third party material.

The parents' role

Although it is true to say that parents or caretakers are merely part of the assessment equation, they are a dynamic factor. Their reaction to being investigated will alter the equation and the social worker therefore has to be clear about how he relates to them. Honesty, authority and compassion should define the relationship: honesty in that the parents have a right to know that they are under scrutiny (the only possible exception to this is in a rare situation where concealing the truth may be necessary to get a child immediately to safety). Authority in that the worker must be secure in carrying out his official duty and in not evading responsibility. Compassion to the extent that, unlike the police, the social worker must be concerned with the interaction between perpetrator and victim.

Parents may be the central source of information about an act of child abuse; it is therefore expedient to seek their co-operation in understanding why the abuse took place. Their willingness may allow more easily the worker to spend time with the child in the home where, despite the abuse, he may feel safer than in hospital room or elsewhere. Parents may appear monsters today but tomorrow they may again have vital things to offer to their child. In the interval the worker has to find ways to leave a door open for negotiation. Parents may only show remorse where they sense a degree of compassion in the worker; without this their hostility and fear may be misinterpreted as cruel indiference and 'lack of co-operation'.

Later in the investigation process, there are further decisions to be made about parental involvement. Should they be invited to the case conference? A study of 38 SSDs (*Community Care*, 12 May 1983, p. 18) found that 22 of them did not invariably inform parents that their child had been placed on the child abuse register and this suggests that the process may firmly exclude parents. The 1986 DHSS Draft Guidelines recommends that parents should be informed but is firmly against their attendance at formal case conferences which they see as 'professional meetings focused on the details of inter-agency co-operation to protect the child and plan for the future' (DHSS, 1986a, para. 2.25, p. 19).

Procedures should provide for both the authority and the compassion roles. A formal fact-finding evidence-sifting meeting may be hampered by the presence of the parents (in the same way that the police do not invite suspect criminals to investigation meetings!) However a subsequent equally formal meeting should be provided so that parents can hear the evidence against them and have an opportunity to reply. Social worker honesty at this stage will help parents to know that a formal process is at work which will at times exclude them. Whether they like it or not, their child's welfare is paramount. This may sound harsh but it is more productive than any attempts to mask the truth. The worker must, at this time, be alert to his own role anxieties. He must investigate firmly and fairly while somehow, often with difficulty, retaining concern for the parents.

Personal qualities and skills

The first prerequisite of the investigator is a high level of *consciousness*, not just about what is taking place objectively and externally, but how he is reacting to a situation and thereby affecting it. This can only flow from a high level of *personal and professional maturity*, from someone who feels equally at home using facts, theory and intuition and can be open to conclusions from either source.

The investigator also needs to be decisive. This is obvious on one level and yet the problem arises because the child abuse work requires high levels of both *contemplation and action*. This is more likely with good support from the agency and supervisor in order to promote a genuine sense of *co-responsibility* that goes beyond merely following procedures.

Finally, the worker needs administrative skills especially in *recording* and *presenting information*, these serve legal, bureaucratic and professional purposes and are essential to protect not only the child and the parents but also the agency and the worker.

Summary

Child abuse investigation has a clear legal basis which puts the child firmly at the centre of the work. However, the reality is that the interests of children and their parents cannot be neatly separated. SSDs carry numerous and unique responsibilities for the protection and care of children and would seem to be the logical setting for investigations.

With responsibility comes power and it is therefore essential that local authority social workers maintain balance to guard against over-wide or over-narrow perceptions of child abuse. During an investigation their role has much in common with the police and this requires the efficient dispassionate pursuit and collation of information from many sources. The condition of the child, the state of the family, their history and their environment are all vital elements to be considered.

Investigation is a process with moments and phases which demand different skills. Timing is important as well as a balance between contemplation and action. The worker will be under many pressures which may lead to misconceptions; these may arise from restricted knowledge, assumptions or personal prejudices. At all times the position of parents presents difficulties; the investigation, centred exclusively on the child's best interests, must be firm and forceful, conducted with honesty, authority and compassion. Using administrative skills helps to translate good investigation by a skilled worker into an assessment that can be used by others and can stand up to the challenge both of self-analysis and of court cross examination.

6

Social Workers as Therapists

Is therapy viable?

So far we have argued strongly for the retention of the role of investigator for social workers, and quite strongly against the role of full-time bureaucrat, by reducing the use of the register machinery. We did not develop these arguments purely for isolated, ethical reasons, although these are important. More importantly, we would like to see the energies of social workers developed and freed for use as therapists in child abuse cases.

Above all, social services departments are large organisations, with many staff who have, collectively, wide-ranging knowledge and skills. If child abuse is a cause for concern, these resources should be made available to produce positive remedies. The 'owners' of these resources should be allowed to apply them for the benefit of clients and not just for the self-protection needs of the agency and staff.

Individual knowledge, skill and energy are resources. This means that they are finite and cannot be devoted in all directions to an infinite degree. If most of the knowledge, skill and energies are devoted to protecting, maintaining and developing bureaucratic systems, the client, quite logically, will get less, or even none of these finite resources.

We suggest, therefore, that serious attempts at therapy require a definite re-allocation of staff resources. This is difficult, but not impossible, and is quite necessary, because there is no indication that effective therapy is being provided, in very general terms, by other agencies or individuals, to an extent which would seriously alter the problem of child abuse as it is generally recognised.

Specialism versus genericism

An apparently easy way out of this dilemma is the creation of special social work therapy teams, because, superficially, at a stroke, the burdens of the bureacratic system can be removed elsewhere. However, we would argue that such arrangements actually reduce the possibilities for inter-departmental co-operation and multi-disciplinary teamwork at a local level by distancing social workers from the networks of information and support which seems to us to be essential to a positive strategy for tackling child abuse. The more predictable forms of abuse would not be adequately dealt with under such a system.

On the other hand, the development of 'patch' systems seems to reduce the level of commitment of time to individuals, which, to us, is an essential ingredient for any attempt at therapy.

The truth, as we suggested in Chapter 3, is that neither specialism nor 'patch' provide total solutions in dealing with the child abuse problem as a whole. Each approach seems to increase disadvantages in one area as a corollary to positive steps in another. For example, the creation of a specialist child abuse unit may enhance the scope for treatment, but the creation of the unit itself may well create distance between all the professionals involved. Conversely, 'patch' systems may enhance detection and information exchange, but demands on time and energy tend to preclude long-term, fixed commitments to individuals except where the social worker delegates tasks to volunteers. Unfortunately, it may be difficult for anyone except a paid, full-time worker to find enough persistence for the really difficult cases.

Neither approach by itself alters the register and associated machinery system. For us it is more important to focus upon this than upon the specialist genericist debate and the main concern of this chapter is perhaps those cases which may arise with little or no warning.

What happens in practice?

In practice, the development of a therapeutic arm – the task culture, in effect – by SSDs in child abuse has been the last stage in development if indeed it has been developed at all. In fact, the almost obsessional dependance upon the child abuse machinery has sometimes worked against the development of imaginative responses. So, in some areas there are no real therapeutic resources, in others a few individual staff have been left to take an initiative, while in other areas other agencies have attempted to fill the gaps, particularly the NSPCC, child guidance clinics and psychiatrists.

Furthermore, where social services departments or their staff have attempted to develop therapeutic resources, these are, to a greater extent, focused upon the adults involved, rather than being directed at the victims of abuse.

This is not to say that a number of social work practices do not have any therapeutic content. For example, the application of the law in a child abuse case may have a therapeutic effect upon the adults or child involved. The obtaining of a resource for a child, such as a childminder, may have a therapeutic effect upon that child. However, in general, such approaches have different goals, and therapeutic effects are largely unplanned, and often unforeseen bonuses in the application of such methods.

We believe that if SSDs are seriously concerned about preventing and ameliorating child abuse, then they are duty bound, even in law, to develop effective, planned therapeutic resources, particularly for the victims of child abuse.

The legal basis for our intervention in such situations quite clearly relies upon the detection and investigation of an unhealthy situation with regard to a child. It also rests on the idea that without such intervention, the 'unhealthy situation' will not improve of its own accord. The logical corollary must, therefore, be the implementation of a therapeutic programme of intervention, because that is the goal that we have taken upon ourselves by invoking the law.

It will be argued that just about everything that is done by social workers in cases of child abuse has a therapeutic content. For example, it might be argued that the punishment of abusing parents is therapeutic because it is a rite of passage for the relieving of guilt that they must feel for their crime. Or, the placement of a severely abused child with loving foster parents will provide that child with what has not been provided by the natural parents.

Any social worker with some experience will know, however, that these assertions are naïve in the extreme. In the examples quoted here the serious psychological harm of punishment or separation is conveniently omitted. In fact, from our own practice, we know and feel that the application of the law and the provision of resources can by themselves often produce as many damaging effects, or even more, than the damage caused by the originally identified problem.

Concentrated therapeutic intervention

When we refer to therapeutic intervention here we are talking about something very distinct and separate from the application of the law, administrative procedures or the provision of child care or adult resources. We are in fact referring to specific programmes of therapy which are directed at the individuals involved in the originally presented problem which attempt to heal the damage caused by such incidents. These are distinct from interventions which attempt to remove the causes of the problem or those geared towards minimising or preventing its re-occurrence.

Significant in our approach is the idea that therapy should be offered to the child victims of abuse which is geared towards removing the trauma produced by abuse, or repairing the emotional damage of abuse, neglect or emotional cruelty.

Traditionally, such tasks have been undertaken by people other than social workers, if they are undertaken at all. We say this because we suspect that in many areas of the country such skills are very sparse or even totally lacking.

We are not suggesting that social workers should be turning themselves overnight into child psychotherapists or the like, particularly where skilled help is already available from other sources. However, generally there is a paucity of such resources and it is glaringly obvious to us that, throughout the history of the development of the child abuse 'industry', therapy for the damaged child is an almost totally neglected area.

At present, social workers have some genuine reasons for not undertaking such work. A preoccupation with the demands of the child abuse register machinery, and lack of training in such areas are obvious reasons for our general non-involvement in therapy, *as well as the other demands of generic work.*

However, we have tried to point a way forward for overcoming the first problem, particularly in Chapter 3. In this chapter we hope to show that the acquisition and use of therapeutic skills is not such a difficult proposition for social workers.

Does abuse harm the child?

This is not a trick question. It is not a play on words. We all must know of children who have, in our eyes, been appallingly treated, and yet there are no signs or symptoms of lasting or even short-term harm. On a more scientific level, studies have shown that in a number of children incidents of clearly defined child abuse have had little or no apparent impact upon the child. For example, a research study into sexual contact between children and adults suggested that a significant number of the children appeared to have suffered no permanent damage as a result of their involvement (Ingram, 1979). This is perhaps not surprising when it is fairly obvious that the child's perceptions of events, actions and relationships were at odds with the views of all of the adults involved.

From our own practice, we are aware of families of more than one child, where there is quantifiable neglect, both physical and emotional, and yet one child will suffer pain and lasting damage and a sibling will not. If we accept the premise of the child as a unique individual, this is perhaps hardly surprising.

We say all this because each case needs to be approached in

a new and fresh way, from a therapeutic point of view. There is no point in applying a detailed therapeutic plan if this is not really needed. We need to be aware of the difference between responding to the nature of the incident, and responding to the needs of a child. To do this we need to be aware of our own feelings and how they are affecting our perceptions and attitudes. Furthermore, we need to be aware of the influence of others on the decisions we may make.

For example, we would cite a case known to us where the offer of support, advice and therapy was made to parents after their child had died at the hands of the father. This was in addition to a prosecution, court appearance and probation sentence for the father. This level of concern and need to be involved in helping the couple sprang directly from the fearful recognition that the family were completely unknown to any helping agency in the period preceding the child's death.

In another example, a new health visitor in a long-running child abuse case was very keen to ensure monitoring help and therapy for the damaged child at the point where everyone else was wanting to curtail involvement. Her own need to maintain this position sprang directly from the identified lack of health visitor input into the family from her predecessor.

We cite these examples because they tend to highlight the lack of real assessment and particularly because they point out the meeting of organisation needs as opposed to client needs. The simple message is that therapy begins from a basis of sound assessment and in each case we do need to question the assumption that what we have identified as child abuse has been harmful to the child.

We accept that this is a very complex task, particularly when we bear in mind that childhood traumas may emerge much later in life, often in temporary or permanent bouts of mental illness. There, therefore, has to be an element of prognosis as well as diagnosis in such assessments. Usually there is a fear about making such predictions, but it is often possible, even in a very young child, to assess personality type and future life chances and expectancies. The idea of prognosis is, therefore, not so strange and should be an integral part of social work, particularly when we consider our legal obligations, both in terms of providing care until the age of 18 (or 19 in exceptional circumstances) and in terms of provision which is focused upon the best interests of the child in question.

Assessment for therapy

Such assessment does not take place in a vacuum, where the sole factor is the need of the child for therapy or otherwise. The decision to undertake applied therapy also relates to the child's situation initially, to his future placement, and to the situation of the proposed worker.

For example, objections from adult carers may preclude real attempts at therapy if we have no legal powers to overrule these objections. It is also potentially damaging to enter into a therapeutic relationship with a child if one cannot make and keep a regular commitment, or if one changes jobs in mid-stream. Such factors are particularly important if we bear in mind that some therapeutic relationships may take a year or two to come to a fruitful conclusion.

There are also dangers within such processes for the child. If we are focusing on traumatic events and helping a child to relive and understand them, there can often be huge emotional or behavioural reactions in the child outside the actual therapeutic contact. These are usually indicative of the depth of damage caused by abuse, neglect or loss and if this is the case with a particular child we must consider whether residential care is not the best situation for such a child, at least in the medium term. If this is deemed necessary, we should be guaranteeing permanency of placement for the duration of the planned therapeutic process.

If we do not achieve this, and the child undergoes one, or a series of moves, we can actually be adding to the pile of neglect, rejection and sense of loss rather than diminishing it. Too often we deal with teenagers who have been traumatised and damaged, not so much by their family, but more by their experience of care.

So assessing the situation to determine therapeutic input is not a static process and does not focus solely upon the perceived needs of the child. It requires a full and realistic appraisal of the present and future environment for both child, worker and agency. Most importantly it requires an honest assessment of whether or not the social worker or other staff are actually up to the job.

Personal qualities of the therapist

So far we have already seen that the ability to commit oneself in a planned manner over a potentially long period of time is one essential ingredient in the therapist. Logically one must also be able to resist pressures to respond to other 'priorities'.

Theoretical knowledge is important, particularly in the areas of child development and depth psychology. However, this is often less important than other 'relationship abilities' and too much conscious concentration can often get in the way of establishing a natural rapport with a child.

Most importantly, perhaps, is the ability to be a child oneself, re-learning how to feel, think and see through the eyes of a child. Social workers who are parents may have natural advantages in some cases, but to rely on this as a necessary trait of a good therapist ignores the fact that we were all children once.

Most of us, most of the time in our client-contact work are used to relying upon and appealing to logical conscious processes as the means of effecting change. It is obvious that if this is our sole mode of working, then we will be seriously limited in trying to establish and maintain a relationship with a child. Relying upon feelings and instincts and a more physical approach, particularly through play, touch or physical care are likely to produce better results, particularly, but not exclusively, with younger children. One case brought to our attention by a colleague makes this point quite dramatically.

In this situation he had been regularly visiting an extremely sullen and uncommunicative boy of 16 in a children's home over a very long period. Each visit was conducted in almost total silence but afterwards the youth's behaviour regressed quite markedly. In one session, for no apparent reason, the boy sat on the social worker's lap for a cuddle, which was given. This was repeated a few times and then the boy asked if he could dress in a nappy and also sit and be cuddled. This did take place and from that point onwards the continual regressions ceased. The boy had been 're-parented' and, having regressed to babyhood, was able to move forward again.

Regression

The need to regress is very evident in many of the children we deal with. Most often it is evidenced in behaviour which is geared unconsciously to the placing of the child or young person in a very child-like, dependent relationship with a significant adult. More often than not we ask people to undertake this latter role who are often ill-prepared for, ignorant of or totally rejecting of the concept of regression. In this context we would place foster parents who often are asked to undertake this task.

Regression implies a need to return to early childhood, and in particular to the point of trauma caused by the terrifying incident whether it be physical harm or emotional neglect, sexual exploitation or outright cruelty. Having re-established the criteria surrounding the original event in the new circumstances, the child or young person will re-enact his part in the episode, usually in the unconscious hope that the reaction of adults will be different this time round. If it is, and is perceived as positive, then the child can begin to develop again because the trauma has been exposed and resolved.

Unfortunately, the response of adults in the new setting is often akin to the original response of the parents in the precipitating situation and, therefore, the child continues not to develop and shows this by continued regressive behaviour.

In one case dealt with by one of the authors, a foster parent injured a young child in his care precisely because he was trying to improve the child's behaviour when in fact the child needed to regress backwards. The incident of injury occurred over the eventual failure of a potty-training programme. Not surprisingly the child continued not to respond to potty training for a further eighteen months. Twice the child experienced rejection by significant adults for behaviour which really needed to be accepted by them at the time as a sign of trust and love.

However, we would be wrong in laying the blame for such occurrences at the doors of people who act as full-time carers. Foster parents in particular are encouraged to think of setting forward goals and achieving them. They can hardly be blamed for feeling depressed, hopeless or frustrated if the child needs to go in the reverse direction.

In such cases there is no reason why social workers cannot undertake such roles, why we cannot attempt to be 'real parents' to the abused children in care, because, stripped of theory, it is this relationship which is at the heart of any successful therapy. Of course, such plans involve real team-work between the therapist/social worker and the full-time carers. For children the process of therapy is largely an unconscious one. Their reactions to therapy can therefore be evident outside the therapeutic setting, and the carers need to understand and accept this, if they are not to work against the therapeutic effort.

Sadly, at the present time such plans are more likely to be evolved between field social work and residential staff than between social worker and foster or natural parents, largely because training and support programmes for the latter groups are, as yet, only slowly developing. However, because a significant number of children still remain in residential care, there is no excuse for therapeutic plans of action not to be implemented for large numbers of damaged children.

The parent-child relationship

The effectiveness of a therapeutic relationship between social worker and child is likely to rely more upon the quality of the relationship than upon the therapeutic 'tools of the trade' applied by social workers in such settings.

Because we are talking here of children who have good reason to fear and distrust adults, we will get nowhere if we do not turn up when we say we will, if we withhold information, are downright dishonest or withdraw from some of the normal human responses to any child, because we fear our own reactions in such situations.

The implementation of a therapeutic plan is therefore a very skilled and serious business, involving a lot of groundwork, particularly with one's colleagues and superiors. They need to understand why it is vital to maintain commitments to a damaged child and support to the therapist/social worker. Without these pre-conditions it is inadvisable to proceed at all, because to fail at the basics of 'parenting the child' may cause more harm than doing nothing.

We may be talking about a number of fixed and immovable sessions throughout each week for some staff, but in relation to some helping professions, this is not an extraordinary move. We also need to leave a lot of time for thought and our own emotional rebuilding and (restoration) after such encounters. If we put ourselves in the role of parent to a number of children, we will be experiencing a wide range of their projections and transferences. These can be painful and confusing and usually the successful therapist will need help in disentangling them. One argument could possibly be that the effective therapist needs to have his own therapist. Alternatively, the use of joint working can spread the load to allow a richer range of therapeutic roles.

Tools of the trade

There is no magical box of tricks which constitutes the successful therapist's tool kit. We firstly must decide which techniques we ourselves feel comfortable with. Children's instincts are usually very finely honed and they can sense falseness, or attempts to be something which one is not. We can extend this into the field of emotional response as well, by saying that honesty of feeling is a desired attribute, and there is nothing wrong in expressing real feeling if it is done in a conscious controlled manner. There might be a tendency, say, not to be angry with a child who has suffered physical abuse, or to withhold affection from a sexually abused child. Whilst these defences are understandable they are, however, counterproductive to the goal of restoring a real and positive relationship between the child and a significant adult.

We come back to the point made earlier about being aware of oneself and one's feelings. Obviously, this is a relative matter, but the social worker undertaking direct therapy can be greatly aided by an objectively based relationship with, say, a supervisor, which is coincident with the therapeutic process with the child.

Such approaches are not new to social work, but their successful application does require, in our view, a reappraisal of the value of casework as a major weapon in our armoury. Perhaps, sadly, skilled practitioners of the art are often no longer in client contact positions. Those that are left are often in senior, training or other non-practising positions. They do need to be identified and encouraged to participate in the support of therapeutic ventures, however, if general headway is to be made in the field of therapy with the victims of child abuse.

Therapeutic theory and the knowledge base

Again there is nothing precious in the art of acquiring therapeutic theory. The base line for such knowledge is located in the internal and external world view of the child. For a young child in particular, such a world is often populated by symbols as tokens of concrete experience for the child. For example, in one case known to us, a child of five described her father as 'a big fat toad in a cage'. Such a description was not only a very clear definition of the father in the child's eyes, but the use of 'toad' also implied something about the child's expectations. It was ascertained through drawings and stories in a number of organised therapy sessions that 'toad' was being used as a universal symbol by the girl, something horrible which could be transformed by love into something highly desirable. The cage represented prison, for this was where the man was. When asked to draw this a number of times, the bars of the cage disappeared over time, as the girl became less afraid to talk about her father with the therapist who was, in fact, a social work student.

Acceptance of the symbolic world is not an easy or comfortable task. In the case quoted above, some colleagues were prepared to accept such interpretations until they began to relate them to their own experiences. At this point they became quite hostile to the approach, and in particular to the symbolism of colour, perhaps because acceptance of such ideas implied that they were more open to interpretation and understanding by others than they thought or hoped for.

Young children often appear to use colours indiscriminately in drawings, and yet, if we accept the symbolic nature of different colours, a lot of sense can be made of their seemingly irrational scribblings. Again, using the case example quoted above, the child's pictures of herself often contained high proportions of black and greys. We took this as a sign of depression and it was interesting to note that over time her use of brighter colours increased as she became increasingly clear about her past, and the role of her often absent father.

Painting and drawing are well-established diagnostic techniques but to make them therapeutic tools there needs to be an active participation on the part of the therapist. If we accept that randomly constructed paintings or drawings are fairly accurate maps of social relationships or internal reality, then we can participate in their construction, helping to transform feelings and perceptions in a therapeutic way.

Donald Winnicott's Squiggle Foundation is based exactly on such an idea.

Winnicott's use, for children in difficulties, of the well-known game – in which one person draws a squiggly line at random and the other person draws over it, turning it into whatever they fancy, and then play being reversed . . . [provides] . . . a lived through experience of spontaneity in relationships, but also, at the same time, provides a record of what has happened which could then be reflected upon and become a way of communicating what can go on in the togetherness of parents and children (Miller, undated).

Play and therapy

The use by children of play and games is well established as a vehicle of learning and socialisation. Jean Piaget's studies in this field are widely accepted as tools for the understanding of a child's development (Piaget, 1948).

With abused children, there are some obvious therapeutic benefits to be gained from play as an approach in itself. For example, the physically abused child may learn through a physical play activity not to fear physical contact with adults. Or the sexually abused girl, say, may learn that there are limits to the development of physical contact through play with a male therapist. Such techniques are not confined to the clinic room, for obvious reasons. Spontaneity of response is one of the keys in therapy. The therapist must always look for opportunities in any situation of contact between himself and the child.

There are some therapeutic play techniques which do not require the active participation of the therapist. For example, sand play and sculpting are individual activities. Their therapeutic value comes from allowing the child to shape and remould or remodel something which again begins as a reflection of concrete internal of experience.

For example, one of the authors watched a young boy on a train as he placed large and small empty beer cans on a table as a map of his family and other significant adults. The boy changed the original layout once, to express his ideal view of his family, then changed them back again to their 'real' positions. In doing this, the boy had expressed a fantasy, and then reshaped it into reality. This simple act of play brought some acceptance of reality and gave an outlet to fantasy. The only thing required of the 'therapist' at this time was to provide a protected space for the 'therapy' to take place.

Play is also useful from the point of view of expediency and efficiency. It provides a quick and relatively tension-free way of establishing contact and can be favourably contrasted with the intellectual or conversational approach which often takes many months to be of effect in establishing rapport. Everyone has or will come across a young person who steadfastly refuses contact on this level, until, after a very long time there is some recognition that the adult really is serious in his or her dedication. Constructing a situation for play can short-circuit this oft-depressing process, and, to extend this, a group at play can add to the speed of the process.

Group therapy

So far, we have focused upon the individual relationship between child and adult, and, for younger children in particular, this is often the best way of proceeding. However, particularly with older children who spend much of their time in groups, the formation of a therapeutic group can often be of great benefit.

However, we would stress a simple formula, that the raising of numbers involved is correlated exactly to the need for increased knowledge and skill. Dealing with groups, particularly where the participants are likely to be very damaged or disturbed, is a hazardous course to pursue, principally because the forces at play in such situations are less under the control of the therapist, are stronger than in one-to-one situations, and are more open to manipulation by the group.

In our view, group therapy with children should only be seen as an extension of individual therapy and needs to be simultaneous with the latter, if it is not to create more damage than it sets out to repair.

This having been said, we feel that the group approach should only be discounted in a positive way, and not because we are afraid of it. We should be aware, however, that the setting up of such processes is largely a matter of pioneering guesswork at present. As Thompson and Khan point out, 'the present position of group psychotherapy could be compared with the early days of psychoanalysis, when Freud's followers were all laying their separate claims to new discoveries and new formulations . . . it would be premature to speak as if coherent schools of thought existed' (Thompson and Kahn, 1970, p. 51).

The biggest danger is that, where, in a one-to-one situation it is relatively easy to re-establish oneself after exposure, in a group this is often a difficult or impossible thing to do, largely because the reactions of a number cannot be guaranteed. However, if the group approach is to be genuinely attempted, we would suggest that therapy is set as a tangential goal rather than an open and specific one. In this respect, a play group, drawing group would be preferred, because the task-centred nature of the group makes it much less threatening to what are already very vulnerable young people.

Timing

If we are really attempting to form a parenting relationship with a child, it is clear that such a process will in all likelihood be a lengthy one. One or two years of regular, perhaps weekly contact, will often be necessary, if the re-parenting goal is to be achieved.

However, the central factor in the length of the process is the exact goal towards which we are working. In some respects, the damage caused can never be completely rectified or removed, so that 'getting better' may be about adjusting to reality rather than changing it.

The therapeutic input may be just one part of an overall plan of action, all, or most of which, falls upon the case social worker. If the child has been placed in care the overall goal may be a successful fostering or rehabilitation home. Usually we feel that these courses of action should be implemented as soon as possible for the sake of the relationships involved. However, we would argue that such plans are unlikely to achieve success if the child is still traumatised as a result of preceding events.

This suggests that some plans may require a lengthy period for implementation, but the ideas that the child could be re-parented by the social worker, alongside lengthy introductions to a foster home, are not as contradictory as they seem. If we accept the concept of projection and transference, then it is logical to assume that once the 'therapist' has rehabilitated the adult–child relationship in which he is involved, then the same process can take place between the child and other 'significant adults'.

The central problem in such an equation is whether or not the adults involved can tolerate such an apparently lengthy process. In effect this highlights the need for an exacting assessment of the adults involved, whether it be foster or natural parents or residential staff.

Finally, it also depends on whether or not the 'therapist' can tolerate the internal stress produced by his dual role as both therapist, with a single task, and as case social worker, with responsibility for the overall strategy. The former requires an exclusive concentration upon the needs of the child. The latter requires an acceptance of the needs of other people involved including foster and natural parents. It will be an unusual situation indeed where not only are these two sets of needs complementary but also where they progress and unfold in a strictly correlated manner. If we are to assume responsibility here we must be brave and skilful enough to walk this particular tightrope. We must also decide whether we are strong enough to maintain balance over a relatively long period.

From all that we have said so far, work with abused children and the adults in their life is a lengthy, demanding business. Therefore any assessment which is going to lead to the drawing up of a plan of action should include an evaluation of the person playing the role of caseworker and 'therapist', alongside an assessment of the other adults involved.

Therapy and the overall plan

So far we have focused almost exclusively upon therapeutic intervention with the abused child. One reason for doing this has been to attempt to redress the balance of work with child abuse in practice, which tends to be focused largely upon the adults involved, whether this is legalistic, bureaucratic, or therapeutic in approach. The other reason was to show that social workers could undertake therapeutic work themselves because the processes are not so mysterious as they might seem, and are not confined to clinics or psychoanalysis.

Of course, for the case social worker, therapy for the child is but one part of his multi-faceted role, and it is only likely to be sucessful if there is an overall strategy with a clear objective.

Too often we are guilty of expressing hopeful and perhaps principled expectations when in reality the facts point to-wards another more effective conclusion. For example, keeping the abused child within his family is too often an expression of hope based on personal belief or agency policy, rather than an attainable target based on scientific deductions from the available facts, when the more effective actions would be removal.

There is little clear-cut guidance to be given in facing such situations. The law asks us to act 'in the best interests of the child', agency policy may dictate reception into care 'as a last resort', liberal ethics may suggest 'minimum intervention', and personal belief may stress the importance of the family. As ever, theory is very contradictory, for over time it has swung towards and then away from the importance of natural parents to the child; at the moment both views seem to be operating with equal but differing vigour.

Perhaps what we should be able to do is to spell out the likely outcome of any course of action which may be taken for any particular child, and then try to be as clear as possible about the factors affecting the eventual decision. This is particularly important in child abuse cases, because these contribute to decison-making meetings, such as public feeling, agency protection and individual self-protection and it is best if these can be included officially in any version of the decision-making process.

Family maintenance or rehabilitation

In compiling this book we advertised in the national social work press for suggestions, guidelines or codes of practice which had been drawn up to provide a structure for assessment in child abuse cares. One offering (which has apparently never been taken up extensively) was appealing to us as an assessment tool, and although based upon critical removal of a child into care, it does attempt, quite bravely, to be explicit about facts to be taken into account in making decisions at every stage. As an effort to conceptualise practice by a field social worker, it is a useful example of what can be produced from 'what we know already'. The author, Neil Macauley (1981), was modest to us about it but we felt that it was very relevant to this part of the book, a volume for practitioners by practitioners.

Treating the abused child is going to be of little value if he is maintained in or returned to a situation where the potential for abuse has not changed at all. We should also understand that punishment of abusing adults by courts, willingness to co-operate with social workers or promises to 'do better' are not in themselves signs of evidence of change. They make us feel more comfortable with or trusting of the adults involved, but we have to decide whether their responses to the child will be any different.

As abuse is usually defined in terms of parental behaviour we are likely to focus upon this as evidence of change. Perhaps it is, therefore, not surprising that behaviour modification techniques have been developed fairly extensively for use by a variety of professionals and that much play has been made of them in the academic field, sometimes to the virtual exclusion of other methods. It seems to us that one of the main advantages of such approaches lies in their benefits to the professionals involved, for their main disadvantage is that there is no guarantee of permanent change. However, there is an appeal to the twentieth-century technocratic mind. 'Measurement of observable, objective facts' is central to the behaviour modification approach. We can, therefore, rest more assuredly in our achievements. However, there is no indication that such approaches modify the trauma of inci-dents of abuse, either for the child, or for the abusing parents or adults. We do not deny that this approach can easily be seen by lay people to be more 'productive' than others. However, extensive reliance upon behaviour modification as the sole therapeutic tool in child abuse is worrying to us because it may be analogous to cosmetic surgery for a serious injury. We would feel happier if it was used in conjunction with other approaches, rather than instead of them. Its merits are that it may allow an early return home of, say, a physically abused child. However, for us that is the beginning of a therapeutic process, not the end of it.

Therapy for abusers

We would not dismiss the idea that a punitive sentence for abusing parents in child abuse cases is necessarily ineffective or harmful to them. In fact, at present the courts are the only forum for the airing of contradictory views, and they have a duty to protect the rights of families from bureaucratic decisions.

Charles argues that,

a good many social workers struggle with their own, and other people's authority, in a way that is unhelpful to their clients. . . . Very few people set out to deliberately injure a child. Where parents have insufficient self control to prevent them damaging their children, they may, at one level, welcome someone else (i.e. the court) providing control for the time being – they hope to enable them, with skilled help, to mature to the point where external controls are no longer needed (Charles, 1983, pp. 19–21).

We do not deny this line af argument, but there are limits to its general application. Most parents are aware that they have done something wrong and will experience guilt and possible depression as a result. Ritualised punishment may help to relieve this, using similar mechanisms to the ones which operate in the confessional and its penance. However, we can only point to the general ineffectiveness of the punitive approach within the general field of criminology, and we know of no reason why the same does not apply in the field of child abuse.

At best, the use of punishment is but one tactic within an overall strategy of help and change, but if it is seen as useful, then ethically the case social worker should be supporting its use instead of leaving entirely such decisions to the police.

We also accept that, in many respects, identified abusers are no different from the 'normal parenting population'. However, the process of identification will have certain practical and psychological effects upon them, which differentiate them as a group. If we are seriously considering keeping a family together, or returning an abused child home, these issues need to be raised and tackled if they are impeding achievement of the desired goal.

Amenable to treatment?

There will be a small group of abusing parents who are felt by most people to be beyond help. We shall refer to these as the 'severely mentally impaired' and the 'psychopaths'. Although in theory we may wish to argue about the suitability of such labels, in practice their use indicates a label of 'untreatability' through all the standard practices of therapy and psychiatry which we would do well to note.

We find a reluctance to concede the applicability of such concepts in academic debate, but a willingness to use them in practice. Ultimately their use implies a termination of the child–parent relationship, either by permanent removal of the child or by incarceration of the adult. Although it seems to go against much of the grain of social work, we know from our practice that such an approach is applicable in a very small number of cases. From a therapeutic point of view, in such cases, the therapeutic effort is and should be directed at the abused child *only*, and *not* towards the parent.

In one case known to us, a father committed incest with his eldest daughter over a long period. It was a very intense and perverse affair.

Its discovery led to his imprisonment, but unfortunately this had no apparent effect upon him and eventually he was back at home with a younger daughter, who was then received into care. The man showed no remorse for his previous activity, other than annoyance at a sentence which had prevented his 'continuing his daughter's education'. He also made it perfectly plain that he would do the same again if *he* thought it was important.

The use of the label 'psychopath' is hardly the central point of debate here. From the 'psychiatric person's' point of view the man was beyond help because his defensive armoury did not allow for anything other than self awareness of need. The decision to remove the child from risk was entirely appropriate as long as ensuing therapeutic intervention helped her to understand the reasons for her position.

If we look at overall illnesses, psychiatry contains the possibility of treatment, and on this basis we would not see the mental illness of a parent being the only reason to invoke the child abuse machinery. However, we must be aware that certain treatments for mental illness actually may reduce the parenting capacity of an adult so we may be thinking of temporary care for a child in this situation. In such cases, the social worker is unlikely to be providing the role of primary therapeutic input for the adult concerned, although in many cases there is no logical reason for this, other than historical tradition. If we are seriously suggesting that social workers can quite adequately undertake the role of child therapist, there seems no reason to us to believe that we could not be equally competent with mentally ill, abusing parents or other adults. This seems quite appropriate when we know that numerous instances of mental illness in adult life are directly associated with unresolved childhood traumas often of the very kind which the adult in question has inflicted upon his/her own child.

However, if the scope for individual therapy for abused young children is quite vast, and thoroughly applicable, the reverse may be true for abusing adults. We would recommend the group approach for adults to be of perhaps more importance, from the point of view of efficiency and effectiveness.

Groupwork with abusing parents

At one end of the groupwork spectrum we have very intense, complex, therapeutic groups such as Gestalt or more recently, psychodrama groups. At the other are those which focus upon the external environment and political factors of child abuse.

> One way would be for social workers to attempt to bring together the abused, the abusers, the abusers' families and social workers in a recognition that abuse is not an individual problem but rather a phenomenon rooted in the structural nature of society. These attempts will de-stigmatise those involved as well as airing and sharing feelings, ideas and support for one another. Collectivising child care may be one outcome of such mutual support, perhaps too the setting up of playgroups, playschemes, as well as women's groups (Popple, 1983).

As is often the case, the answer, at least for us, lies somewhere in between. Groups for abusers could be extremely useful as mechanisms for overcoming the sense of isolation, guilt and depression which most abusing parents feel. Support, advice and warnings from peers may also be much more acceptable than from 'alien beings' such as social workers. However, we would not go so far as to suggest that social workers should attempt to hide their true roles and positions within such groups, for the retention of the authority and leadership roles within the group is nothing more than a reflection of the position outside the group (with the individuals concerned).

In practice, most groups which we know that function for adults are run by social workers and operate not with child abuse as a principal or sole reason for their existence, but for some other reason which it is hoped may have a bearing upon the reoccurrence of abuse.

For example, in our own locality, two groups operate with actual or potential abusers, but they are ostensibly geared towards meeting other needs and directed at other goals. Interestingly, they are both run for women, by women, and we suspect that this is generally true across the country. This is perhaps rather alarming when we consider that male abusers are either as prominent as women, or more so in certain forms of child abuse, but perhaps this does nothing more than point to the fact that such groups already in existence do not focus solely or even largely upon child abuse as the criteria for membership.

There is no reason why groups could not be focused upon child abuse, either run directly by social workers, or on self-help lines, such as Parents Stress Anonymous. Such groups could be primarily educational or 'training' focused, and some group models may well be quite suited, given simple changes in content. For example, modification of the contents of foster parent training courses might provide a suitable tool for dealing with abusers, particularly where their children have been removed temporarily from them.

In any such group the revelation within the group of continued abuse may have serious repercussions for the individual outside the group, particularly if social workers are running or participating in the group. We should, therefore, think very hard about proposals for therapeutic groups modelled along Alcoholics Anonymous lines. This all points to the need to be very specific at the outset about the function and rules of the group, as well as being aware that individuals within a group are in touch with many more potential resources than they would be in isolation. For example, a group provides its members with a number of opinions, a quantity of advice and a level of empathy which may be absent between an adult and a social worker. It also has the potential for exploring a number of alternative child care resources which, if used properly, provide a means of avoiding the statutory care path.

Work on an individual level

Despite the attractiveness of behaviour modification techniques as an intervention tool with abusing parents it is clear that their use by social workers is scattered and fragmentary. We detect an unwillingness on the part of some social workers to look actively at these techniques, either on moral grounds or from the point of view of lack of skill or expertise, but if nothing else, this denies the reality of everyday social work practice, for most of us use these tools, albeit in an unconscious or unplanned way.

If social workers argue against the use of behaviour modification techniques on moral grounds, we feel it is incumbent upon them to propose alternative techniques for combatting child abuse which can match the apparent success rate of behaviour-modification. To date we can only detect a rather deafening silence over this; this again reinforces our view that most energies in social work have gone into role culture development, leaving individual practice in its infancy.

If the problem about their usage is more to do with lack of knowledge or skill, then we would suggest taking a short cut to the fonts of wisdom by approaching psychologists, or more recently, a group such as community psychiatric nurses. For those who wish to tackle the problem themselves, from first principles, we would suggest a few basic readings, with *Child Abuse – a Study Text* by Vida Carver (1978) as a good basic beginning.

If, for whatever reason, this approach is consciously

rejected as inappropriate in dealing with abusing adults, then we are left to fall back on the more traditional approaches of social work, psychoanalysis or psychiatry. We should remember, of course that the adults in question usually are in a position to accept or reject offers of therapeutic help and, likewise, have the ability to choose between certain approaches. Too often failure to take up the help that is offered is seen as lack of willingness to co-operate, whereas poor presentation or denial of choice may be the real reasons for lack of positive action.

Honesty about child abuse goes much further than providing information about the law, bureaucratic procedures and the rights of parents in respect of them. It also includes a definite statement of belief that someone does need, and can benefit from, help and in addition, a statement about what the best form of help might be and the grounds for this assessment.

Social workers as resources' gatekeepers

For a variety of reasons social workers as individuals may not be in the best position to provide the help that is needed for abusing parents. For this reason we have a moral legal duty to ensure that other resources are available and that we know something of their actual or potential efficiency in a given situation. (The next chapter is especially concerned with the relationship between local authority social workers and these 'other' resources.)

An essential range of departmental resources should include domiciliary support through family aides and day staff who have a high level of theoretical understanding and a wide range of appropriate skills. It is not necessary for departments to provide other resources, but social workers should be aware of and be able to link families easily with child guidance clinics, those with defined therapeutic skills and with the wider range of psychiatric resources. They should also be able to identify gaps where they exist and then come up with definite strategies for the filling of these. Similarly, an SSD which develops positive volunteer programmes will increase its therapeutic armoury. Although this chapter has concentrated on the social worker as therapist, it should be an axiom of the work that help usually requires different and complementary skills at more than one level. A far from recent account by Davies (1977) showed how volunteers were often more effective than social workers at building therapeutic relationships with the families of handicapped children. Holman makes the same point eloquently in insisting that throughout his community project his co-leader was an untrained young man who had been 'through the mill' himself (Holman, 1981).

If nothing else, the general public and abusing parents themselves expect us to be good 'child welfare' departments. Admittedly, there is an element of self-protection in ensuring that such resources are available and accessible, but in the true spirit of therapy we should do nothing which helps those responsible for an action to be able easily to shift the responsibility for it to someone or something else. If we are to be successful in tackling child abuse we have a duty to look after ourselves as important resources. Defences against the inappropriate shifting of responsibility are quite in keeping with this ethos as far as we are concerned.

Summary

One of our primary intentions in this chapter was to attempt to redress the balance of what we perceive to be the current focus of practice in the field of child abuse. This is the reliance upon organisational procedures instead of positive therapeutic intervention, and a focus upon child victims of abuse, as opposed to the habit of dealing largely with the adults involved.

We have also tried to suggest that social workers are in a position to provide such therapeutic help and that this is in keeping with the other roles as investigator and co-ordinator.

We have touched upon therapeutic techniques which have tended to be, but need not be the sole domain of the trained psychotherapist. We have suggested that abuse which leads to trauma and then regression demands the process of re-parenting if we are to ensure that the child's proper development is not being 'avoidably prevented or neglected'.

We have not omitted therapeutic interventions with the abusing adults concerned, but we have suggested that the normal practice of individual counselling and support needs to be re-examined in the light of groupwork theory and models used for other groups in day-to-day social work practice.

Overall, we would ask that social workers should look upon themselves as positive resources, drawing upon the large pool of untapped skills and resources which already exist amongst our colleagues and within ourselves. If any of these things are to happen SSDs need to 'release' their front-line staff as much as possible from pressures which discourage imagination and creativity. Therapy ought to involve experiment, exploration and individual risk-taking. If child abuse work is seen to be an important social work task SSD management must create organised opportunities for practitioners to develop skills which are to do with treatment as well as procedures.

7

Strategies for Tomorrow

The last chapter of a book should be the most important. It is the acid test for both authors and readers where two lonely questions emerge. 'What has been demonstrated so far?' and 'What can people take away that will actually be useful?' It is not so difficult to be critical, not so easy to offer constructive alternatives, but a practical book in a practical series has to do just that. Yet we tread a tightrope here, for sometimes a simple exhortation to do may in fact be simplistic and may merely encourage practitioners to think that solutions are self-evident. Psychiatrists face similar problems if they rely over-much on chemotherapy and take little account of the family, and social and other environments which affect their patients' responses; on the other hand, people learn best by doing and they, therefore, need models for action. A misguided guide can, in fact, be the quickest method of discovering what the problems really are.

This might *all* sound like 'an apology in advance', a form of insurance in case the book is a disappointment to readers. We hope not for we intend it more as a preface to *our first assertion* in this chapter, namely that for local authority social worker child abuse is not amenable to easy answers. We have reiterated our feeling that a practical guide for 'doing' child abuse work is not possible for two reasons: firstly, because the syndrome may not be as distinctive as others have sometimes argued; secondly, and consequently, there is no specialised approach that will have much impact. In fact, attempts to isolate child abuse from the mainstream of family social work may have led us up a blind alley. If anything, then, practical

121

guidance will only make a contribution if it can persuade practitioners (and their managers) to reconsider, to regain perspective and to open their attitudes to some of the exciting wider movements that could improve work with families.

Our second assertion is that the local authority role will not easily allow social workers to become child abuse specialists. The SSD will continue to have a cradle-to-grave mandate to implement government policies and this constraint has, in our view, always lurked beneath the surface particularly when it comes to the hard question of allocating *real* resources. For all the furore, child abuse work in SSDs has always been short of funding especially in areas like research and post-qualifying training.

Obstacles to child abuse work

Before we can develop ideas about how local authority social workers might tackle child abuse in the future, we need to be clear how they are doing it now. What are the central beliefs? What are the essential styles and methods of work? We see three key features which we shall discuss in turn: Multiple Roles, Uncertain Professional Status and Methods of Work and Isolation.

Multiple roles

We have already explained the widely accepted dilemma of the social worker in combining the roles of investigator and helper. There is no escape from this dilemma, therefore any guide to action has to take it into account. Is it possible to arrange things in an SSD so that perhaps individual staff can be allowed to adopt either one role or the other? Could we envisage a system where perhaps the frontline local social worker is largely relieved of investigating and then taking onerous action about child abuse; where a second tier of workers moves in to pursue the legal processes of protection and care?

Let us not pretend that this issue is easy to resolve. In our view it is one which, above all others, makes patch system proponents sound woefully unconvincing if not downright evasive. A curious thing about local authority social services work is the persistent refusal of some people to accept the reality of the setting. We have heard social work academics argue that they train students for social work not for working in SSDs; this is no better than making raincoats out of tissue paper. Perhaps the hardest thing for the new social worker in a local authority is the shock of responsibility, of duty and of accountability to a wider social system.

What is perhaps remarkable is that so many social workers cope with role conflict in their jobs. To do this requires a level of sensitivity, insight and knowledge which ought to encourage us. Perhaps we should also be heartened that in Britain we retain a tradition both realistic and humane, which says in effect that the state has to undertake painful duties but there is room within them for compassion and individual care. If so, then a fusion of often contradictory roles is possible. Important research by Sainsbury *et al.* has studied long-term family work by local authority social workers, probabtion officers and family service unit workers.

One of their more interesting findings was that clients seem to cope quite well with the exercise of authority by their workers. They say, for example:

> In the analysis of replies for sub-groups of families, we found that 'statutory' cases were proportionately more highly represented in the 'friendly' categories than were 'voluntary' cases (excluding the four families in the probabtion voluntary group), in the clients' reports, but not the workers'. Similarly, families' levels of active dislike towards social workers were lower in the 'statutory' groups. This phenomenon was not recognised by the workers, however, who appeared to have accepted the common but untested assumption that 'voluntary' clients relate more readily to their helpers (Sainsbury *et al.*, 1982, p. 123).

Later on the authors suggest, 'In short, therefore, it was in statutory work that workers seemed most sensitive to the risks of being too firm with their clients and they appeared on the whole to exaggerate this risk' (p. 131).

Perhaps the problem is not so much that social workers

carry authority but rather that they are uncomfortable with it and may be tempted to dilute or disguise it. One of the authors recalls a client whose care of her children had to be investigated. After an initial period of anger and fear she eventually admitted that it would have been even worse if the social worker had not come clean about the purpose of his visit. She *knew* she was going to be investigated and she said she was, therefore, relieved not to be given 'all that crap about coming to see how I was coping with the kids'.

Carrying authority is a fact of life – for parents, teachers, policemen and social workers. Just as it has always been a feature of the work so it will continue. Different SSDs may make various structural arrangements for allocating executive authority but it will always permeate the social worker's life. As we suggested in Chapter 3 the most important issue is that the SSD reorganises the pressure it exerts on practitioners and makes proper arrangements for skilled sensitive support by supervisors. Basic training courses for their part must devote time to role conflict theory and the material we offer in the Appendices sets out the key contexts and concepts.

Inappropriate expertise

The disease model of child abuse has had the dangerous effect of suggesting to social workers that if they can become expert therapists armed with intricate themes of early psycho-social development and detailed knowledge of complex family and marital relationships, they can do sophisticated long-term work with abusing families.

How realistic is this and does it happen in practice? Does social work training offer the knowledge base for this to be possible? The Barclay Report (1982), among others, appears not to believe this. Its general descriptions of the work done by social workers do not cast social workers as expert therapists and its recommendations for one-to-one work stop cautiously at the basic counselling role. Thus Jordan has expressed similar reservations recently: 'I would maintain very strongly that very few bits of social workers' knowledge or skills are unique. What's unique to social work is it has to have a great range of non-unique bodies of knowledge and skill with which it has to be able to work *reasonably well'* (our italics) (Jordan, 1984, p. 10).

We have referred ealier to the range of roles occupied by social workers. Jean's analysis of roles found that work in the area of changing clients behaviour (the classic therapeutic position) was surprisingly infrequent (Jeans, 1978) and Sainsbury *et al.* came to similar conclusions in discussing 'insight' work. Hence 'the only thing that makes these [insight] techniques particularly contentious is that their use is currently debated at abstract ideological and political levels, where they are seen as wholly 'good' or wholly 'bad' without reference to the experiences, needs and lives of service – users' (Sainsbury *et al.*, 1982, p. 70). Mayer and Timms (1970) in their classic study also convey a picture of clients who weren't always aware they were being 'caseworked' and had other goals in mind anyway!

How does this argument square with our earlier chapter on 'the social worker as therapist?' Are we saying that, from the evidence, social workers are really deluding themselves if they think they are offering therapy to child abuse clients? As usual we have to take a middle line and suggest that practitioners use whatever themes and techniques appear helpful yet retain a realistic view of what is possible. The intensity of child abuse work opens up a vast arena for interpersonal work and in the previous chapter we attempted, but only broadly, to suggest some considerations. However, social workers should seriously consider that they might be pushed beyond their knowledge base at times; if so they should swallow their pride and call in workers who may be more skilled. Where this is not possible they need to root their therapies in the wider context as Jenkins argues in the case of family therapy (Jenkins, 1984, pp. 12–14).

There is a trend in some SSDs to promote child care specialisms. Will this produce better therapists for child abuse? We doubt it for the reasons that Jordan develops in the paper we have quoted.

Local authority social workers are stubbornly generic in their methods whatever some people may think. They operate a wide range of techniques, through a series of roles, in a range of circumstances '*reasonably well*'. Later on in this chapter we shall try to suggest how this generic pattern can go on developing. For the moment it is perhaps right to say that the true knowledge base for local authority social workers lies in the application of concern for individual through a working relationship within the local authority setting.

Isolation

It may seem surprising to talk of social workers being isolated in a field where, as Stevenson (1980) has said, the three C's – communication, co-operation and collaboration – have dominated so much past and present thinking. Yet we are preoccupied with a picture of the social worker ploughing a very lonely furrow in child abuse work. The isolation seems to occur at the level of the actual work with the client; at another level, that of inter-professional communication through the case conference, there appears to be much support, yet we know from experience how lonely and threatened prac- titioners feel. The isolation seems to stem partly from the exclusiveness of the investigator role with its heavy responsi- bilities and also from the still dominant one-case-one-worker ethos of social work.

By and large social workers do not share cases with colleagues, nor do they make much use of volunteers and others. Sainsbury *et al.* comment on this (1982, p. 93) and the major study by Holme and Maizels (1978) also identified a preference for using volunteers in a compensatory rather than complementary way, hence not as true co-workers. The alarmed conferring of profesionals on a child abuse case has sometimes produced a kind of protective muddle which discourages truly co-operative working.

The 'Key-worker' concept may exaggerate the social worker's sense of isolation with its implication that the practitioner is responsible for the whole management of the case, for the whole client. We can contrast this with the medical model and the relationship for example between general practitioner and hospital surgeon; both would see clear domains in which they work and accept responsibility while yet sharing the treatment of the patient. Yet one of the curious features of SSDs is the way the accountability pointer moves up and down the hierarchical scale so erratically. At times it is the whole department which accepts responsibility, at others the director or senior staff and at others the frontline practitioner. Confusion can breed isolation and the caring, responsible social worker may too often have to adopt the gloomy view that the buck stops with him.

Thus, we would identify isolation, in terms of individual perceptions in hierarchical reality and in methods of work, as a strong feature of child abuse work. Anxiety tends to draw in workers' horns, make them play safe and try to keep everything under their personal control. This may be counter-productive. Figure 7.1 sums up our view, because at a time when the child abuse crisis will need intervention on many levels, social workers may find themselves walled in and unable to collaborate easily.

Developing child abuse work

The remainder of this chapter is based on two propositions:

1. For the local authority social worker, it is abuse within known families rather than unanticipated and unsual situations elsewhere which is the major challenge and
2. Child abuse work can be best improved by retaining and expanding the generic role.

We have been particularly influenced by the following authors/works: Pelton (1981a) and his views on the social context of child abuse in America, Parton (1985) who has applied similar arguments to the British scene, Pancoast *et al.* (Froland, 1981) for their work on helping networks, Whittaker and Garbarino (1983) with their broad ecological model, the Home-Start Programme (Van Der Eyken, 1982) (particularly in Leicester) and Holman (1981) for his local voluntary work on a Bath housing estate.

Pelton argues caustically:

The mystique of psychodynamic theories has captivated many helping professionals, who seem to view the espousal

128

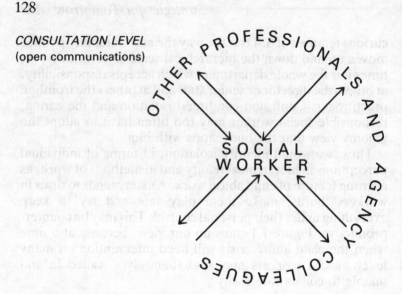

CONSULTATION LEVEL
(open communications)

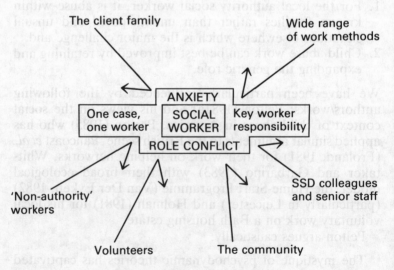

INTERVENTION LEVEL
(restricted communication)

Figure 7.1

and practice of such theories as conferring status and prestige upon themselves. Unfortunately, the mundane problems of poverty and poverty-related hazards hold less fascination for them. . . . Although concrete services are the ones most attractive to prospective lower-class consumers, they are the services that are least appealing to the middle class helping professionals immersed in the 'phychological society' (Pelton, 1981b, p. 31).

To illustrate this simply, one of the authors recalls asking a young local authority social worker, six months after her qualifying training course how she was finding her work. 'It's all money and housing', she replied wearily.

Continuing this theme of the narrow or the wide view of social work Garbarino has said:

Americans typically see the solution to social problems in pairs of people, when they move beyond the individual at all. Whether the problem be child abuse, alcoholism, teenage pregnancy or violence in schools, we 'naturally' adopt a dyadic model for dealing with the phenomenon. Victim-perpretator, pusher-user, teacher-student – our understanding of the problem is always shaped by the notion that behaviour is best understood as the interaction of individuals (Garbarino, 1981, p. 233).

It is perhaps a possibility that America which led the way in 'discovering' child abuse, may now, 25 years later, be struggling towards a new perspective. We can also predict that Britain may follow, although we suspect that because, here, the links between statutory investigation and voluntary therapy have remained within SSDs there is need for a less drastic change of direction.

However, our view is that, for local authority social workers it is the bottom end of society which causes most concern about child abuse and therefore preventive work should aim broadly at this group's total life circumstances.

The ecological model

System theory in social work should, by now, be a thoroughly rooted perspective. The notion that people and their activities form inter-connected systems which may require a variety of interventions offers a modest but useful structure, at least for considering people and their problems. If this idea is linked with the concept of ecology – the study of people's adaptation to their total environment as it affects the quality of life – then we have a broad conceptual platform for locating as issue like child abuse.

Within this concept Whittaker and Garbarino (1983) have written at length of the ecological approach in social work. Their latest work ranges over the whole of welfare services and urges a social work approach based on the belief that we can identify or map the features, people and relationships which constitute a person's ecological environment and then work to strengthen various parts of it in various ways. Essentially, it envisages working 'in' and 'with' rather than 'at' clients, co-ordinating the skills of others and developing the statutory/voluntary/neighbourhood continuum.

Ecosystems

Whittaker and Garbarino draw on Bronfenbrenners' earlier work in defining four systems within the environment:

The Microsystem: the close, immediate, day-to-day sum of experiences, relationships, settings of an individual.
The Mesosystem: consists of links and relationship processes between microsystems, the way in which, for a child, experiences and people at home and at school are linked.
The Exosystem: this in effect is someone else's system over which the individual may have no control, but which have an important effect on him. For example the case conference in relation to the abusing parent.
The Macrosystem: the broadest level, 'the broad ideological and political patterns of a particular culture or sub-culture'. For example, the sum of society's views about child abuse will ultimately influence all other, lower systems (Whittaker and Garbarino, 1983, pp. 11–15).

How could the above model help a social worker better to understand a child abuse case? Esentially, it is in an aid to mapping the contexts of the abuse, for putting it in a wide perspective.

We might find for example that the abusing parents had either few or many *microsystems* – friends, relatives, neighbours – for all too often abusing families lack such systems (the classic isolated family) or it may be there are important close contacts, which are unhelpful: grandparents whose negative attitudes increase stress on the parents, may distort perceptions of the world; a depressed housing environment which generates violent fearful living in its residents. Alternatively, we might identify microsystems that have potential to help, the neighbour down the road who actually likes the abusing mother, the sympathetic shopkeeper or another parent in difficulty.

The linkage and interplay of systems *(the mesosystem)* may be worth exploring, for the social worker, the shopkeeper and the friendly neighbour could perhaps be encouraged to combine their efforts. The social worker may need to seek out a local policeman who is currently in touch with the abusing family so that they can improve their liaison and co-operation. The aggregate of various microsystems might give clues about the pattern of the family's interests and needs. It might appear that there are serious conflicts between different microsystems, thus between a mother's role as daughter (to her parents) and as wife (to her husband) which are damaging her ability to cope with her children. Often a problem for abusing families is that they will be visited (or at the very least reacted to) by different individuals; where this patchwork of microsystems is not linked then stress, misunderstandings and multiple goals can arise. (A classic example from another area of social work is where residential workers may complain after a child returns from home leave that 'the family have undone all our good work!')

Exosystems are particularly important in child abuse. Of these, perhaps it is the case conference which most menaces the abusing parents in the way that it makes recommendations which are then implemented by the social worker who is part of the client's microsystem. At the same time another exosystem, the local housing authority, may be deciding that it is time to put pressure on the family to reduce their rent arrears. A change of policy in the local police force may, simultaneously, mean that abusing parents face a greater risk of prosecution.

We find the distinction between systems in which one participates, and those of others, a useful one to get a better feeling about the various pressures which impinge on a family. The social work task with exosystems may be as critical as with microsystems. If the practitioner works patiently to encourage and extend good relationships and contacts for the client, yet neglects the activities of outside factors, his work may be hampered or even nullified. In addition, the social worker needs to be aware of the difference between his own micro- and exosystems. Thus he may need the help of a senior colleague in liaison work with other agencies, again a matter of work-sharing with cases. In turn his supervisors need to be sensitive to this potential difficulty; if the social worker feels alienated from his agency, sees it as an exosystem, he may be less equipped to act as agency representative in investigating child abuse and in making proper detached judgements about case-management.

For the client, a sense of threat and isolation can arise if he sees a world full of unsympathetic exosystems which menace his family life. While the social worker cannot necessarily bridge this gap he needs to consider exactly how they influence his client. An exosystem may become subjective rather than objective – 'all the people on this estate hate us' – and clients may actually exclude themselves where it might otherwise have been possible to develop a microsystem.

It may not always be clear where the exosystem stops and the *macrosystem* begins. Whittaker and Garbarino suggest that a macrosystem is harmful when it

threatens to impoverish people's microsystems and mesosystems, and set exosystems against them. It can be a national economic policy that tolerates or even increases the chances of economic dislocations and poverty for families. . . . It can be a pattern of demands and reinforcements that tolerates or even aggravates conflicts between the roles of worker and parent (Whittaker and Garbarino, 1983, p. 14).

If a government becomes concerned about levels of violence, emphasises the moral responsibility of parents and also encourages a tougher policy against offenders it can subtly reduce sympathy for abusing parents and harden the attitudes of people who encounter them. An economic policy which reduces aid to blighted urban areas may sap the morale of local residents and reduce the range of interpersonal relationships and support networks.

Working across the exosystem

We can use the above model to explore the implications for social work in child abuse. What is implied is a concerted effort at various levels by various staff, professional and otherwise. If we drew up a strategy for an SSD, it could be illustrated as in Table 7.1.

Table 7.1

System	Worker	Objective	Example
Macrosystem	Senior staff	Influencing and creating helpful ideologies at local and national levels	Corporate Management Group (Chief Officers) advocacy resource allocation
			Lobbying Government ministers (individually and through Association of Directors of Social Services)
			Sitting on national advisory bodies
			Public relations work through the media, lectures, etc., to 'educate' the public
			Formal liaison or other agency chiefs (e.g. joint funding)
			Devising SSD policies to create a more helpful department climate for child abuse work

Table cont. p. 134

System	Worker	Objective	Example
Exosystem	Middle staff	1. Influencing agencies who impinge on abusing families 2. Implementing systems and strategies to support practitioners	Formal liaison with local chief of other agencies. Joint development of partnership schemes with community groups, voluntary agencies Managing and monitoring SSD relationships between practitioners and other staff in the department. Overseeing liaison with magistrates, police Public work at local level (with training and research staff) organising training courses for practitioners, initiating data systems on both clients problems and the outcome of treatment methods Ensuring adequate personal supervision for practitioners
Meso- and Microsystems	Practitioner staff	1. Identifying client systems. 2. Enhancing helpful systems 3. Acting as link with exosystems	Developing assessment skills to identify helpful and harmful networks for clients Developing one-to-one therapeutic relationships with clients Seeking, promoting and co-ordinating helpful networks Linking the work of other professionals Explaining to clients the influence of exosystems – especially the menacing ones e.g. court and police system Occupying and making clear different microsystems in which the social worker/client relationship may vary according to circumstances

We hope we have shown, if only in outline, that an SSD can develop a total strategy for child abuse. Too often in the past, in answer to the question 'What is your department doing about child abuse?', senior staff have been limited to saying, 'We have tightened up our procedures and written guidelines for practitioners'. Whittaker and Garbarino devote two long chapters (and three more, concerned with school, ado-lescence and delinquency) to exploring such an approach in detail. Similarly Froland *et al.* 1981 make wide-ranging proposals aimed at a wider community approach and they even attempt to cost such work.

Sexual abuse – in ecological terms

We can develop our ideas further by being even more specific and concentrating on an aspect of child abuse which has attracted growing interest in recent years. Sexual abuse as a problem that merited its own heading in At Risk Registers seems to date from the late 1970s. Despite the original DHSS decision (subsequently reversed, 1986a) not to include it as a separate category, a large number of SSDs have, in fact, done so, including as many as 75 per cent of respondents in a survey in 1983 (*Community Care*, 12 May 1983, p. 18).

In America, there have been extreme reactions to sexual abuse. Speaking to the Merseyside BASW Branch in Summer 1983, a visitor from Washington DC, USA, outlined that state's efforts to discover, record and treat victims. The State's definition of sexual abuse 'did not require touch. Obscene telephone calls, showing pornography and indecent exposure were included in the definition' (Muir and Gegg, 1983, p. 4).

In 1984 revelations about wholesale sexual abuse of children in a California pre-school nursery seem to have sparked off a nationwide panic. Widespread television cover-age cries 'epidemic' and professional workers everywhere may be tempted to rush in with instant action and the kind of crisp, simple answers that the public prefers to hear.

In this country Erin Pizzey, then of the Chiswick Family Rescue, was reported at the 1980 BASPCAN Conference as being 'terrified' that the DHSS proposals omitted sexual abuse from their list of register headings (Pizzey, 1980, p. 5).

We have an impression that sexual abuse concern largely reflects the 'disease model', wherein sick caretakers are perpetrating sordid acts against children. It would follow that treatment would mainly aim to identify individual and family pathology and attempt to cure the offenders or remove the child. We might even speculate about the influence of the feminist movement and its strong and punitive recommendations about rape, on current views of sexual abuse. Yet paradoxically, in a sombre *Sunday Times Colour Supplement* report (2 September 1983) on mass murders there is a clear implication that social conditions seem to be producing this bizarre breed of criminal and that individual therapy may make little headway with them until after their inexplicable crimes have been committed.

An exosystem approach to sexual abuse will clearly not exclude individual therapy with the parents. However, it may enable us to ask other questions and to consider other approaches. For example, what is the sexual ethos of the parents' relationships outside their marriage? How do their friends discuss sex? What about the husband's work colleagues? Do they regularly read pornographic magazines? What about newsagents which stock such magazines? What is the government view about the commercialisation of sex?

It seems clear to us that sexual abuse does not happen in isolation. If a father, fed on a diet of bizarre 'blue movies' made available through local contacts, acts out some of his fantasies on his 8-year-old daughter, where should the work begin? The social worker could perhaps set up discussion groups among mothers which could also help to reduce the isolation of the abusing parent. Local community figures could perhaps help in a campaign against the worst examples stocked in local shops. The abusing father might need individual help in understanding how crude humour and role expectations at work affect his attitude towards sex within his family.

The important thing, in our view, is that the social worker should take the broad view. We prefer this to anything that smacks of yet another witch-hunt against 'a sick minority'; better a flexible response that acknowledges both the complex psychology of family sexual relationships and their social context.

The wider view – examples in practice

Although we have relied heavily on American literature, there is encouraging evidence of important pioneering work in Britain. The examples we quote have a common theme – that professional workers can benefit by identifying and working through helping networks of various kinds; this does not mean handing over responsibility for statutory work. Rather it represents attempts to discover the various levels and methods which every case demands.

If we think of exosystems we need to consider the potential for different agencies collaborating more at local level. Holman reports an attempt by Kirklees Metropolitan Council to improve its services to a high risk estate. In April 1983 a decentralised office opened on the estate staffed by social work education welfare health visitor housing and environmental health staff. In the first nine months there were 6339 calls of which 68 per cent concerned housing, repairs, and financial queries and 11.3 per cent were for social work help (Holman, 1984, p. 11). If the various agencies can ensure that they communicate regularly there seems much potential here for the social worker to monitor and even influence systems which clearly impinge on clients. There is a lesson here for SSDs which are developing patch systems. It may be less profitable to set up unilateral local offices without consulting other agencies who might have more frequent contact with social problems.

Lay therapists and others

Lyons has described a London SSD team which has developed a patch approach. Her report includes an interesting description of work done with an at risk family:

A socially isolated mother, lacking in confidence, had to care for three children alone while her boyfriend was in prison. A similar situation previously had resulted in her hitting the children, attempting suicide, and the children being admitted to care for 15 months. This was avoided a second time by the social worker helping the woman develop a network of sympathetic people to whom she could turn (Lyons *et al.*, 1983, pp. 17–18).

The network included the local headmistress, a neighbour, a volunteer who provided a babysitting service, a voluntary organisation which provided a holiday for the children and the local church and its playscheme. Thus the family's microsystems were increased and enriched and the social worker (we assume) was instrumental at the mesosystem level as a vital link and co-ordinator. We have a picture of a rich network of support for the mother, the interplay of differing roles and skills and, most important, the client playing an increasingly active role at the centre.

Holman's work on a Bath council estate has become (or should be), well-known and his main account gives a vivid and human picture of truly local voluntary work. A constant theme of his book is the importance of using non-professionals because they are seen as less threatening, they know the local scene, they speak the right language and in many cases they have been through the same problems themselves. He also makes the point that clients more often seek basic counselling, consisting of comforting listening and guiding, rather than therapy (Holman, 1981, p. 93). Sainsbury *et al.* (1982, ch. 4) made a similar point in identifying the importance to clients of encouragement from their helpers.

What is striking from the account of Holman's work is the generic theme. He says that social problems come in all shapes and sizes and fluctuate over time and that responses and worker skills need to be equally flexible. If there is a dominant theme, it is tolerance, openness and compassion, rather than a single method of intervention which has come up trumps.

'Home Start'

We have referred earlier to Van Der Eyken's (1982) account of an experiment in Leicester to develop a system of long-term intensive voluntary work with young families. Put very briefly, the scheme established a Home Care Organiser who recruited local volunteers, operated an open-door policy regarding referrals, worked with families with serious problems, seemed able to retain its volunteers for a long period, and seems to have had some success.

The value of this account is that it describes general helping skills within local networks yet also has a psycho-dynamic philosophy; for example, the author has a useful chapter on reality therapy which acknowledges the importance of the close one-to-one relationship between client and worker. However, the richest harvest comes in the chapters which record the diaries of volunteers working with two cases over a long period. It is here we get the flavour of the potential of skilled voluntary work with clients whose children have been at risk. What also carries across is the volunteers' appreciation of the local authority social worker role and their attempts to interpret this to the clients.

It may be argued that the commitment of the Home-Start volunteers was exceptional and is not, therefore, a reliable guide. Social workers often complain that investing in volunteers brings poor returns and that it is quicker and safer to do it themselves. It may be that intermediaries such as Home Care Organisers may be needed to maintain a structure for reliable work.

Nevertheless, the Home-Start report does argue persuasively that at risk families can receive effective help from workers who lack professional qualifications. As such it is worth further study.

Groupwork in ecological terms

Abusing parents are often isolated. They may also be resistant to individual help from the social worker who will inevitably symbolise, partly at least, authority and threat. We can seek to multiply and enrich such parents' microsystems in various ways, some of which we have outlined above. Lay therapists may often be able to tread where social workers are forbidden, using both counselling skills as well as their local contacts to extend the helping network. A good example of this is given in the Home-Start account of 'Carla' and her children', social network diagrams at the beginning of contact and again nineteen months later show a dramatic increase in relationships as well as an improvement in her perceptions of official figures (Van Der Eyken, 1982, pp. 155 and 157).

The best work acknowledges that one-to-one relationships may not always be enough or may sometimes be inappropriate. They may need to be supplemented by group experiences and these can be sought in two ways.

Firstly, we can seek or create 'sympathetic' groups for those people who share a certain problem. This offers a number of advantages:

- reassurance (that there are others like you)
- common basis for membership (all abusers)
- explicit purpose (to talk about child abuse)
- commitment to therapy (or else why join the group?)
- clear social worker role (he convened the group)

If parents can be persuaded to join such a group it can offer them the opportunity to confront some of the painful realities which follow from discovering that something has gone wrong and they are in trouble with the authorities. This may also help the social worker clarify his double role and explore some of the therapeutic possibilities discussed in the previous chapter.

A disadvantage of a therapeutic group is the very discomfort of knowing you 'have a problem'. It is common knowledge, and not difficult to achieve, that the group setting can encourage the expression of strong feelings. What is not always recognised is that group members may leave group sessions in a state of agitated isolation. Once feelings are ventilated a group needs a sense of movement, direction and most important of all, an idea about the limits of the process. How much has to be done before the group terminates, what constitutes success and is there some kind of finishing line? Thus, a therapeutic group needs clear statements, either from the leader or through collective agreement, about targets; otherwise individuals may simply become a mass of expressed but unresolved tensions.

emain an arm of the state and exercise vital protective
unctions; like parents they will never simply be friends with
heir 'children'. Protection involves difficult skills that have to
>e learnt in order to confront pain and hostility.

However, to continue the parental analogy, it is important
hat parents do not operate in isolation. A child's micro-
ystems need to be linked – the home, school, friends and
'elatives – and the most successful parents do not claim a
nonopoly of skill and influence over their children. We also
1ave to learn that apparently undesirable influences cannot
:asily be ignored. Holman's work on 'inclusive' and 'exclu-
,ive' foster parents, namely those who encouraged the child's
inks with the natural family and those who resisted, conclu-
led that such links are valuable (Holman, 1980). A Darting-
on study of 450 children in care comes to a similar conclusion
ind remarks on the persistence of the children's loyalty to
heir natural families (Millham, 1985).

Whether investigating allegations or acting as parents,
ocal authority social workers need to avoid working in
solation. Children at risk inhabit a complex world and as
Jarbarino argues:

> The process by which a neighbourhood's character affects
> child maltreatment is threefold: the high level of neediness
> inhibits sharing; the lack of positive models reinforces
> inappropriate and inadequate behaviour; the lack of inti-
> mate and confident interaction inhibits nurturance and
> feedback (Garbarino, 1981, p. 24).

While this summary may not explain or encompass *all*
ncidents of child abuse it is wide enough to give a theoretical
ind practical framework for local authority social workers; a
framework within which they might provide protection and
:are fairly, calmly and humanely. The Beckford Report made
much of the unique role of SSDs:

> the making of a care order invests Social Services with
> pervasive parental powers. By such a judicial act society
> expects that a child at risk from abuse by its parents will be
> protected by Social Services personnel exercising parental

powers effectively and authoritatively on behalf of society. Such a child is a child in trust (Beckford Report – Conclusions, p. 297).

This is firm and salutory. Its only weakness, and a crucial one, is that it portrays SSDs as custodians not partners in a task which, we believe, has no experts and has no narrow answers.

Appendix A

Glossary of Legal and Administrative Provisions

Area Review Committees   Local organising advisory and monitory bodies set up in 1974 following DHSS circular. Consist of senior representatives of the Local Authority (Chief Executive, Education, Social Services and Housing Departments) the Area Health Authority, medical staff and nursing and health visiting staff, police, probation and the NSPCC.

ARCs' task was to set up machinery to deal with child abuse, to keep records, monitor work and promote training and information.

1986 DHSS Draft Guidelines propose that ARCs will be re-named: henceforth as *Joint Child Abuse Committees* which will report to *Joint Consultative Committees* (local and health authorities) in each area.

Balance of Probabilities   The basis for decisions made in juvenile court care proceedings about children at risk. Different from criminal proceedings where a higher standard of proof and evidence is required.

Care Proceedings   Juvenile Court proceedings (Sections 1 and 2 Children and Young Persons Act 1969) whereby children aged 0–17 years may be brought before the court in their own interests. Proceedings can be brought by SSD, (most commonly), police, Education Authority, or the NSPCC. Only the SSD and Education Authority are duty-bound in this respect.

Care Order   An order available in care proceedings vests responsibility for children in the local authority (SSD) which then has power to make arrangements for care. These powers supersede those of the parents except in matters of marriage, religion or emigration.

Case Conferences   *Advisory* meetings to consider information and make recommendations relating to specific child abuse cases. Set up following

147

1974 DHSS circular. Attendance is normally limited to official agencies and staff.

Department of Health and Social Security (DHSS)   The government department responsible (in England and Wales) for the work of Local Authorities, Personal Social Services and Health Authorities.

Has issued important circulars which *recommend* policies and practice in child abuse (see Appendix B).

Guardian ad litem (GAL)   A person appointed at the discretion of the juvenile court in care proceedings (and adoption, parental access to children, appeals against parental rights resolutions, and (indirectly) custodianship applications). Created by Children Act 1975 but not fully implemented until 1984. The GAL's duty is to safeguard the welfare of children by making *independent* enquiries, reports and recommendations to the court.

Health Visitor   Employed by Area Health Authorities and most often attached to General Practitioners' surgeries. Have a legal duty to carry out developmental checks on young children. Have no legal right of entry to homes.

'Home-on-Trial'   A practice term used to describe the arrangement whereby children subject to care orders are allowed to live with their parents (Section 21(2) Child Care Act 1980). The SSD retains full power to terminate or vary this arrangement.

Informants   Individuals who make allegations of abuse by others. Their identity can be concealed following a House of Lords ruling in 1977.

Investigations   The SSD has a duty (Section 2(1) CYP Act 1969) 'to cause enquiries to be made' if they receive an allegation of child abuse. The NSPCC has a similar *power* but not a duty.

National Society for the Prevention of Cruelty to Children (NSPCC)
A charitable organisation founded by amalgamation in 1889. Has the power to investigate child abuse and to bring children before a juvenile court in their own interests.

Place of Safety Order   A legal provision (Section 28(1) Children and Young Persons Act 1969) to remove a child in an emergency to a place where he will be safe. Application can be to a single magistrate by (normally) SSD or police and can last for up to 28 days. During this period the SSD has full control of the child.

Police   Have a general duty to investigate crime and prosecute offenders. Have the power to investigate child abuse and bring care proceedings. Have power (Section 28(2) Children and Young Persons Act (1969) 'to detain a child or young person' without application to a magistrate for up to eight days.

Powers of Entry SSD has no power of entry in the homes of children. *But* under Section 40(3) of Children and Young Persons Act 1933 the police have power to execute a magistrate's warrant to search for and remove a child.

Prevention SSD has a duty (Section One, Child Care Act 1980) to provide services to promote the welfare of children by reducing the need for them to come into or remain in care or appear before a court.

Registers A system of local recording of children at risk from abuse, recommended by 1974 DHSS Circular. Registers to be arranged by ARCs and maintained by SSDs, Health Authorities or the NSPCC. 1986 DHSS Guidelines recommend that registers should be re-titled Child Protection Registers.

Supervision Order A provision (Section 11 Children and Young Persons Act 1969) for the supervision of children 0–17 years at home. Can include various conditions including regular medical examinations. Refusal by the parents to comply could consitute grounds for a Place of Safety Order.

Wardship High Court provision (Section 7(2) Family Law Reform Act 1969) by which *any person* with a legitimate interest in a child may apply for that child to become a ward of the court. Once the application is in process the child's location and care cannot be changed until the case is heard. Once a Wardship order is made, the High Court retains responsibility for the child.

Appendix B
DHSS Major Circulars and Guidelines

1974 LASSL (74)(13)   *Non-Accidental Injury to Children*
Offered recommendations on the diagnosis of child abuse and the organisation and management of local services.
   Recommended the creation of ARCs, central register systems and case conferences.

1976 LASSL (76)(2)   *Non-Accidental Injury to Children: Area Review Committees*
A review of progress made since the 1974 circular. Included examples of various ARC child abuse procedures.

1976 LASSL (76)(26)   *Non-Accidental Injury to Children*
The Police and Case Conferences
Recommended the inclusion of police in case conferences. Approved the disclosure to conferences of criminal records of adults living with or likely to associate with children. Recommended more flexible police policy on the prosecution of abusers.

1980 LASSL (80)(4)   *Child Abuse: Central Register System*
Recommended the definition and extension of Register categories to include: physical injury; physical neglect; failure to thrive and emotional abuse; children in the same household as a person previously involved in child abuse.
   Also recommended that children's names be placed on or removed from the Register only by case conference decision.

1986   Child Abuse – Working Together (draft guidelines)
Attempted to summarise and re-define local policy and practice. Offered *broader* defintion of child abuse as: physical injury; neglect; emotional ill-treatment; sexual abuse; potential abuse.

Recommended that Registers be re-titled Child Protection Registers.

Recommended that ARCs be re-titled Joint Child Abuse Committees which should report to Joint Consultative Committees (which oversee joint planning and collaboration between local authorities and health authorities).

N.B.   For full information the circulars and guidelines should be read. In addition, a useful discussion is provided in N. Parton, *The Politics of Child Abuse*, 1985, pp. 102–14.

References

Baker, E., Hyman, C., Jones, C., Kerr, A. and Mitchell, R. (1976) *At Risk: An Account of the Work of the Battered Child Research Department* (NSPCC), London, Routledge & Kegan Paul.

Barclay, P. (1982) *Social Workers: Their Role and Tasks*, London, Bedford Square Press.

Beckford Report (1985) *A Child in Trust (The Jasmine Beckford Enquiry Report)*, London, Borough of Brent.

Bentovim, A. and Bingley, C. (1985) 'Parenting and parenting failure: some guidelines for the assessment of the child, his parents and the family' in British Agencies for Adoption and Fostering, *Good-enough parenting*, pp. 45–57.

Bergman, A. B. (1980) 'Abuse of the Child Abuse Law' in Cook and Bowles (eds) (1980) p. 84.

Borland, M. (ed.) (1976) *Violence in the Family*, Manchester, Manchester University Press.

Bradshaw, (1972) 'The Concept of Social Need' in *New Society*, 30 March, p. 34.

Brearley, C. P. (1980) *Admission to Residential Care*, London, Tavistock.

Brearley, C. P. (1982a) *Risk and Aging*, London, Routledge & Kegan Paul.

Brearley, C. P. (1982b) *Risk and Social Work*, London, Routledge & Kegan Paul.

Briggs, T. L. (1980) 'Research on Interprofessional Social Work Teams in United States of America' in Lonsdale, S., Webb, A. and Briggs, T. L. *Teamwork in the Personal Social Services and Health Care*, London, Croom Helm, pp. 36–8.

Brill, N. (1976) *Teamwork: Working Together in the Human Services*, New York, J. B. Lippincott.

British Association of Social Workers (BASW) (1982) *Child Abuse Enquiries*, Birmingham, BASW.

British Association of Social Workers (BASW) (1985) *Policy on the Management of Child Abuse*, Birmingham, BASW.

British Association of Social Workers (BASW)/Health Visitors Association (1983) 'Joint Statement' in *Social Work Today*, 25 January.

152

British Medical Association (BMA) (1981) *The Handbook of Medical Ethics*, London, BMA.

Brown, T. (1983) 'A Switch in Emphasis' in *Community Care*, 12 May, p. 35.

Brown, T. (1984) Personal communication.

Brunel Social Services Organisation Research Unit (1974) *Social Services Departments: Developing Patterns of Work and Organisation*, London, Heinemann.

Carver, V. (ed.) (1978) *Child Abuse – A Study Text*, Milton Keynes, Open University Press.

Challis, D. and Davies, B. (1980) 'A New Approach to Community Care for the Elderly' in *British Journal of Social Work*, vol. x, pp. 1–18.

Charles, J. (1983) 'Dangerous Misconceptions' in *Community Care*, 1 December, pp. 19–21.

Chisholm, B. A. (1980) 'Questions of Social Policy – A Canadian Perspective' in Cook and Bowles (eds) (1980) p. 367.

CIBA (1984) (Foundation Study Group), *Child Sexual Abuse within the Family*, London, Tavistock.

Cook, J. V. and Bowles, R. T. (eds) (1980) *Child Abuse: Commission and Omission*, Toronto, Butterworths.

Cooper, C. (1985) 'Good-enough, border-line and bad-enough parenting' in *Good-enough Parenting*, London, BAAF, pp. 58–80.

Cooper, D. M. (1982) in Glastonbury, B., Cooper, D. M. and Hawkins, P., *Social Work in Conflict: The Practitioner and the Bureaucrat*, Birmingham, BASW, ch. 7.

Coventry NSPCC (1983) Annual Report, Coventry, Child Abuse Unit (NSPCC).

Creighton, S. J. (1984) *Trends in Child Abuse*, London, NSPCC.

Creighton, S. J. (1985) *Child Abuse in 1983 and 1984, Research Briefing No 6*, London, NSPCC.

Currie, R. and Parrott, B. (1981) *A Unitary Approach to Social Work – Application in Practice*, Birmingham, BASW.

DHSS (1974a) *Report of the Committee of Inquiry into the Care and Supervision Provided in Relation to Maria Colwell*, London, HMSO.

DHSS (1974b) *Non-Accidental Inquiry to Children*, LASSL (74) 13, London, HMSO.

DHSS (1975) *Report of the Committee of Inquiry into the Provision and Co-ordination of Services to the Family of John George Auckland*, London, HMSO.

DHSS (1976a) *Non-Accidental Injury to Children: Area Review Committees*, LASSL (76) (2), London, HMSO.

DHSS (1976b) *Non-Accidental Injury to Children: The Police and Case Conferences*, LASSL (76) (26), London, HMSO.

DHSS (1980) *Child Abuse: Central Register Systems*, LASSL (80) (4), London, HMSO.

DHSS (1981) *Child Abuse: A Study of Inquiry Reports 1973–81*, London, HMSO.

DHSS (1983) *Children in Care in England and Wales 1983*, London, HMSO.

DHSS (1985a) *Review of Child Care Law*, London, HMSO (Inter-Departmental Working Party).

DHSS (1985b) *Inter-departmental Working Party Report for Review of Child Care Law*, London, HMSO.

DHSS (1985c) *Social Work Decisions in Child Care*, London, HMSO.

DHSS (1986a) *Child-Abuse – Working Together* (draft guidelines), London, HMSO.

DHSS (1986b), Social Services Inspectorate, *Inspection of the Supervision of Social Workers in the Assessment and Monitoring of Cases of Child Abuse when Children Subject to a Care Order have been Returned Home*, London, HMSO.

Dale, P., Davies, M., Morrison, T. and Waters, J. (1983) *A Systematic Family Therapy Approach to Child Abuse*, Rochdale, NSPCC Special Unit.

Dartington Social Research Unit (1983) *Place of Safety Orders*, Bristol University/Dartington SRU.

Davies, M. (1977) *Support Systems in Social Work*, London, Routledge & Kegan Paul.

Devon Social Services Section (1978) *NAIC Co-ordinating Meeting Study – January–June 1978*, Exeter, Devon County Council.

Devon County Area Review Committee (1984) *Child Abuse 2nd Edition*, Exeter, Devon County Council.

Dingwall, R., Ekelaar, J. and Murray, T. (1983) *The Protection of Children*, Oxford, Basil Blackwell.

Ditchfield, J. (1986) 'Child Homicide and Child Physical and Sexual Abuse' in *Research Bulletin No 18* (Home Office), London, HMSO.

Egan, G. (1980) *The Skilled Helper*, 2nd ed., Monterey, Calif., Brooks/Cole.

Fahlberg, V. (1981) *Attachment and Separation*, London, BAAF.

Franklin, A. W. (1975) (ed.) *Concerning Child Abuse*, Edinburgh, Churchill Livingstone.

Franklin, A. W. (1983a) Lecture at *Community Care* Conference, London, May 1983.

Franklin, A. W. (1983b) 'Lessons in the last decade' in *Community Care*, 12 May, pp. 39–40.

Fry, A. W. M. (1981) 'Assessment in Child Abuse' in *Child Abuse and Neglect* (USA), vol. v, pp. 159–65.

Froland, C., Pancoast, D. L., Chapman, N. J. and Kimboko, P. J. (1981) *Helping Networks and Human Services*, London, Sage.

Garbarino, J. (1981) 'An Ecological Approach to Child Maltreatment' in Pelton, L. H. (ed.) (1981) (*see below*) p. 233.

Gelles, R. J. (1980) 'The Social Construction of Child Abuse' in Cook and Bowles (1980), p. 342.

Gilmore, S. (1973) *The Counsellor in Training*, New York, Prentice-Hall.

Gorell Barnes, G. (1984) *Working With Families*, London, BASW/Macmillan.

Hadley, R. and Hatch, S. (1981) *Social Welfare and the Failure of the State*, London, Allen & Unwin.

Hadley, R. and McGrath, M. (1980) (eds) *Going Local*, (NCVO Occasional Paper I), London, Bedford Square Press.

Hadley, R. and McGrath, M. (1984) *When Services are Local – The Normanton Experience*, London, Allen & Unwin.

Hall, M. H. (1975) 'A View from the Emergency and Accident Department' in Franklin, A. W. (1975), p. 10.

Hallett, C. and Stevenson, O. (1980) *Child Abuse: Aspects of Inter-Professional Communication*, London, Allen & Unwin.

Harlesden Community Project Team (1979) *Community Work and Caring for Children*, Ilkley, W. Yorks., Owen Wells.

Hilgendorff, L. (1981) *Social Workers and Solicitors in Child Care Cases*, London, HMSO.

Holman, R. (1980) 'Exclusive and Inclusive Concepts of Fostering' in Triseliotis, J. *New Developments in Foster Care and Adoption*, London, Routledge & Kegan Paul, pp. 69–84.

Holman, B. (1981) *Kids at the Door*, Oxford, Basil Blackwell.

Holman, B. (1984) Report in *Community Care*, 23 August p. 11.

Holme, A. and Maizels, J. (1978) *Social Workers and Volunteers*, London, Allen & Unwin.

Home Accident Survey (1982) *The Home Accident Surveillance System*, London, Board of Trade.

Home Office (1984) *Criminal Statistics for England and Wales 1984*, London, HMSO.

House of Lords (1978) Judgement in D vs NSPCC (1978) 1 All ER 589 76 LGR 5HL, pp. 546–624.

Ingram, Father M. (1979) in *British Journal of Medicine*, January/February 1979.

Jeans, M. S. (1978) *Role Analysis in Field Social Work: the Development of a New Model*, Exeter, Devon Social Services Department.

Jenkins, H. (1984) 'Too Hot in the Kitchen' in *Social Work Today*, 7 May, pp. 12–14.

Jordan, B. (1984) Interview in *Social Work Today*, 3 September, pp. 10–14.

Kadushin, A. and Martin, J. A. (1981) *Child Abuse, An Interactional Event*, New York, Columbia University Press.

Kakabadse, A. (1982) *Culture of the Social Services*, Aldershot, Gower.

Kempe, R. S. and Kempe, H. (1984) *The Common Secret: Sexual Abuse of Children and Adolescents*, New York, W. H. Freeman.

Lee, C. M. (ed.) (1978) *Child Abuse – A Reader and Source Book*, Milton Keynes, Open University Press.

Lynch, M. A. and Roberts, J. (1977) Predicting Child Abuse: Signs of Bonding Failure in the Maternity Unit, *British Medical Journal*, vol. i, pp. 624–6.

Lyons, K. *et al.* (1983) 'Our Crowd' in *Social Work Today*, 13 December, pp. 17–18.

Main, A. and Gegg, A. (1983) 'Say no and tell someone' in *Social Work*

Today, 19 July, p. 4.

Maple, F. F. (1977) *Shared Decision Making*, London, Sage.

Marriott, R. (1983) NSPCC Special Unit, Plymouth, Devon, personal communication.

Mayer, J. E. and Timms, N. (1970) *The Client Speaks*, London, Routledge & Kegan Paul.

Millham, S., Bullock, R., Hosie, K. and Haak, M. (1985) (Dartington Social Research Unit), *Children Lost in Care*, Aldershot, Gower.

Miller, M. *The Sqiggle Foundation – a pamphlet* available from The Squiggle Foundation, 19 Chalcot Road, London NW1 3LL.

Moore, J. (1983) Lecture to *Community Care* Conference, London, May.

MORI (1985) *Child Abuse: A Research Study on Behalf of Gamble and Milne*, London, Market and Opinion International Ltd.

NSPCC (1982) *Annual Report 1982*, London, NSPCC.

NSPCC (1983) *The Centenary Charter*, London, NSPCC.

NSPCC (1984) *Developing a Child-Centred Response to Sexual Abuse*, London, NSPCC.

NSPCC (1985) Report in *Social Work Today*, 16 December, p. 4.

Nelson-Jones, R. (1982) *Theory and Practice of Counselling Psychology*, London, Rinehart, Holt & Winston.

Nelson-Jones, R. (1983) *Practical Counselling Skills*, London, Rinehart, Holt & Winston.

Nursing, Midwifery and Health Visiting Professions (1982) Joint Report, London, December.

Oliver, J. E. (1977) Reports to Parliamentary Select *Committee on Violence* in the Family (see below), vol. i, para. 24, p. x and vol. II, p. 159.

Oliver, J. E. (1983) 'Dead Children from Families in N.E. Wiltshire' in *British Medical Journal*, no. 286, pp. 115–17.

Packman, J., Randall, J. and Jacques, N. (1986) *Who Needs Care? – Social Work Decisions about Children*, Oxford, Blackwell.

Parliamentary Select Committee (1977) *Violence in the Family*, HC 329, London, HMSO.

Parsloe, P., Stevenson, O. *et al.* (1978) *Social Service Teams: The Practitioner's Viewpoint*, London (DHSS), HMSO.

Parsloe, P. (1981) *Social Services Area Teams*, London, Allen & Unwin.

Parton, N. (1985) *The Politics of Child Abuse*, London, Macmillan.

Payne, M. (1982) *Working in Teams*, London, BASW/Macmillan.

Pelton, L. H. (1981a) (ed.), *The Social Context of Child Abuse*, New York. Human Science Press.

Pelton, L. H. (1981b) 'The Myth of Classlessness' in Pelton (1981a), p. 31.

Pfohl, S. J. (1980) 'The Discovery of Child Abuse' in Cook and Bowles (1980), pp. 323–40.

Piaget, J. (1948) *The Language and Thought of the Child*, London, Routledge & Kegan Paul.

Pizzey, E. (1980) Reported in *Community Care*, 20 May, p. 5.

Popple, K. (1983) 'Not an Individual Problem' in *Community Care*, 15 December, pp. 18–19.

Richardson, R. (1984) Personal communication.

Rutter, M. (1975) *Helping Troubled Children*, Harmondsworth, Penguin.

Sainsbury, E., Nixon, S. and Phillips, D. (1982) *Social Work in Focus*, London, Routledge & Kegan Paul.

Seebohm Committee (1968) *Report of the Committee on Local Authority and Allied Personal Social Services*, London, HMSO.

Sharman, R. L. (1983) *Child Abuse – A Discussion Paper* London, Council for the Education and Training of Health Visitors.

Shearer, A. (1979) 'Tragedies Revisited' in *Social Work Today*, 16 January, p. 14.

Sheridan, Dr M. (1975) *Reports on Public Health and Medical Subjects*, no. 102, rev. ed., London, HMSO.

Sheppard, M. (1982) *Perceptions of Child Abuse: A Critique of Individualism*, Norwich, Social Work Today/University of East Anglia.

Short Report (1983) *Report of the Parliamentary Social Services Committee, On Children in Care*, vol. 1, HC 360–1.

Skinner, A. E. and Castle, R. C. (1969) *78 Battered Children – A Retrospective Study*, London, NSPCC.

Smith, G, (1980) *Social Need, Policy, Practice and Research*, London, Routledge & Kegan Paul.

Smith, G. and Ames, J. (1976) 'Areas Teams in Social Work Practice: A Programme for Research' in *British Journal of Social Work*, vol. vi, pp. 43–70.

Smith, S. (1975) *The Battered Child Syndrome*, London, Butterworth.

Stevenson, O. (1980) Lecture to the British Association for the Study and Prevention of Child Abuse and Neglect (BASPCAN) reported in *Community Care*, 20 March, p. 5.

Thompson, S. and Kahn, J. H. (1970) *The Group Process as a Helping Technique*, Oxford, Pergamon.

Thorman, G. (1982) *Helping Troubled Families*, New York, Aldine.

Van Der Eyken, W. (1982) *Home-Start – A Four Year Evaluation*, Leicester, Home-Start Consultancy.

Weir, Dr K. (1983) 'On the Defensive' in *Community Care*, 20 January, p. 16.

Whittaker, J. K. and Garbarino, J. (1983) *Social Support Networks: Informal Helping in the Human Services*, New York, Aldine.

Index